PENGUIN (🐧) LIBERTY

ON IMPEACHMENT

Corey Brettschneider is a professor of political science at Brown University, where he teaches constitutional law and politics, as well as a visiting professor of law at Fordham University Law School. He has also been a visiting professor at Harvard Law School and the University of Chicago Law School. His writing has appeared in *The New York Times*, *Politico*, and *The Washington Post*. He is the author of *The Oath and the Office: A Guide to the Constitution for Future Presidents*, two books about constitutional law and civil liberties, and numerous articles published in academic journals and law reviews. His constitutional law casebook is widely used in classrooms throughout the United States. Brettschneider holds a PhD in politics from Princeton University and a JD from Stanford Law School.

ON IMPEACHMENT

The Presidency on Trial

EDITED WITH AN INTRODUCTION BY
COREY BRETTSCHNEIDER

SERIES EDITOR
COREY BRETTSCHNEIDER

PENGUIN BOOKS

PENGUIN BOOKS
An imprint of Penguin Random House LLC
penguinrandomhouse.com

LIBRARY OF CONGRESS CATALOGING-IN-PUBLICATION DATA
Names: Brettschneider, Corey Lang, editor.
Title: On impeachment : the presidency on trial /
edited with an introduction by Corey Brettschneider.
Description: New York : Penguin Books, 2020. | Series: Penguin liberty |
Includes bibliographical references. |
Identifiers: LCCN 2020011834 (print) | LCCN 2020011835 (ebook) |
ISBN 9780143135104 (paperback) | ISBN 9780525506782 (ebook)
Subjects: LCSH: Impeachments—United States—History—Sources. |
Presidents—Legal status, laws, etc.—United States—History—Sources.
Classification: LCC KF5075 .O5 2020 (print) | LCC KF5075 (ebook) |
DDC 342.73/062—dc23
LC record available at https://lccn.loc.gov/2020011834
LC ebook record available at https://lccn.loc.gov/2020011835

Printed in the United States of America
1 3 5 7 9 10 8 6 4 2

Book design by Daniel Lagin

Contents

ON IMPEACHMENT

Part I: ORIGINS OF IMPEACHMENT   1

Part IV: BILL CLINTON   115

Series Introduction

On November 9, 1989, the Berlin Wall fell. Two years later, in December 1991, the Soviet Union collapsed. These events, markers of the end of the Cold War, were seen by many as the final triumphant victory of democracy over authoritarianism and communism. Political scientist Francis Fukuyama famously declared the era to be the "end of history," suggesting that Western-style liberalism was the ultimate form of human ideology. There was a strong consensus—at least in the West—that liberal freedoms were necessary in any society.

But since then, that consensus has been shaken. In the twenty-first century, democracies have crumbled across the globe, with authoritarian leaders grabbing power and eroding traditional rights protections. Examples abound. Mexico and the Philippines embarked on extrajudicial drug wars; Nicolás Maduro's regime brought a state of near-famine onto Venezuela; Poland's Law and Justice Party functionally turned parts of the media into its propaganda arm. In countless other countries, leaders have impinged on citizens' freedom. Even the United States—where liberal freedoms have often been taken for granted—has faced powerful movements and leaders who have disputed the legitimacy of the very rights that underpin our democracy.

Yet in the United States, calls to restrict rights have always run up against a powerful adversary, one that dates back to the country's founding: the Constitution of the United States. This Penguin Liberty series is designed to explore the Constitution's protections, illuminating how its text and values can help us as modern citizens to reflect on the meaning of liberty and understand how to defend it. With rights-based democracy under attack from all angles, it is crucial to engage in ongoing discussion about the meaning of liberty, its limits, and its role in the modern world.

Certainly, the ideal of liberty has been present in America since the dawn of the American Revolution, when Patrick Henry reportedly declared, "Give me liberty, or give me death!" In 1776, the Declaration of Independence proclaimed liberty an "unalienable Right"—along with "life" and the "pursuit of Happiness"—enshrining it as a central American aspiration.

These statements, however, are only a start in thinking about liberty. Mistakenly, they seem to suggest that liberty is absolute, never limited. But in this series, we will see that idea continually challenged. Various liberties sometimes conflict, and we must deliberate among them. Importantly, the liberty to be free from government intervention, or what the British philosopher Isaiah Berlin called "negative liberty," must sometimes be balanced against our liberty as a democratic people to govern in the general interest, an idea he called "positive liberty." Thus, the series will also emphasize the importance of liberty not only in terms of freedom from government intervention, but also as self-government, the freedom of all of us collectively to decide on our own destinies.

Ratified in 1788, the Constitution was an attempt to codify the high ideal of liberty as self-government. Through intense debate at the Constitutional Convention, a document was forged that limited government power and gave people a say in how they were to be governed. Its goal was to "secure the Blessings of Liberty to ourselves and our Posterity." Still, many Americans were not convinced the Constitution went far enough in protecting their individual freedoms from government coercion—what Berlin would call "negative liberty." Although the push for a Bill of Rights failed at the Constitutional Convention, the First Congress ratified one in 1791. These first ten amendments to the Constitution focused largely on securing individual liberties.

Just over 4,500 words long when originally passed, the U.S. Constitution is the shortest written governing charter of any major democracy. Its brevity belies its impact. Ours is the world's longest surviving written constitution. Some scholars estimate that, at one time, as many as 160 other nations based their constitution at least in part on the U.S. Constitution. The United Nations Universal Declaration of Human Rights from 1948 overlaps significantly with provisions of our Bill of Rights. Individual freedoms that our Constitution champions inspire peoples across the globe.

Of course, the original Constitution protected liberty for only a restricted few. As written in 1787, the Constitution did not explicitly outlaw racialized chattel slavery. Almost 700,000 black people were enslaved in the United States at the time of its founding, a fact that the Constitution did nothing to change and tacitly allowed. Article I prohibited Congress from outlawing the international slave trade until 1808, and the three-fifths clause cemented Southern white political power by having enslaved people count toward political representation without allowing them to vote.

Not all the framers wanted the Constitution to be tainted by slavery. James Madison and Alexander Hamilton, for example, thought slavery morally wrong. But they were willing to compromise this conviction in order for Southern states to ratify the document they so cherished. Thus was born

America's original sin, a legally sanctioned system of racial op-pression that persisted formally until the Civil War. Only after an estimated more than 600,000 Americans gave their lives in that bloody conflict was the Constitution amended to outlaw slavery, guarantee "equal protection of the laws," and establish that race could deny no citizen access to the franchise.

Enslaved Americans were not the only ones left out of the original Constitution's promise of liberty. Women were guar-anteed no formal rights under the Constitution, and they were deprived of equal political status until 1920, when suffragists finally succeeded in amending the Constitution to guarantee women the vote. In the Founding Era, the vote in many states was restricted mainly to white male property owners.

These significant failures are reasons to criticize the Con-stitution. But they should not lead anyone to discount it alto-gether. First, the Constitution has demonstrated a remarkable resilience and capacity for change. In each of the cases de-scribed above, the Constitution was later amended to attempt to rectify the wrong and expand citizens' rights. Second, and perhaps more important, the Constitution's deepest values have often inspired and strengthened the hand of those seek-ing justice. That's why Frederick Douglass, himself a former enslaved person, became an ardent supporter of the Constitu-tion, even before the passage of the post–Civil War amend-ments that ended slavery and provided equal rights. In his Fourth of July oration in 1852, he praised the Constitution as a "glorious liberty document," but added a crucial caveat: it protected liberty only when it was "interpreted as it ought to be interpreted." Douglass believed that while many saw the Constitution as a pro-slavery document, its text and values supported broad protections for freedom and equality.

Douglass's point, though delivered more than 150 years ago, inspires this Penguin Liberty series. The Constitution is not a static document. Nor is it just a set of provisions on paper.

The Constitution is a legal document containing specific rules, but it also gives voice to a broader public morality that transcends any one rule.

What exactly that public morality stands for has always been up for debate and interpretation. Today, after the passage of the post–Civil War amendments, the Constitution takes a clear stand against racial subordination. But there are still many other vital questions of liberty on which the Constitution offers guidance without dictating one definite answer. Through the processes of interpretation, amendment, and debate, the Constitution's guarantees of liberty have, over time, become more fully realized.

In these volumes, we will look to the Constitution's text and values, as well as to American history and some of its most important thinkers, to discover the best explanations of our constitutional ideals of liberty. Though imperfect, the Constitution can be the country's guiding light in dark times, illuminating a path to the recovery of liberty. My hope is that these volumes offer readers the chance to hear the strongest defenses of constitutional ideals, gaining new (or renewed) appreciation for values that have long sustained the nation.

No single fixed or perfectly clear meaning of the Constitution will emerge from this series. Constitutional statements of liberty are often brief, open to multiple interpretations. Competing values within the document raise difficult questions, such as how to balance freedom and equality, or privacy and security. I hope that as you learn from the important texts in these volumes, you undertake a critical examination of what liberty means to you—and how the Constitution should be interpreted to protect it. Though the popular understanding may be that the Supreme Court is the final arbiter of the Constitution, constitutional liberty is best protected when not just every branch of government but also every citizen is engaged in constitutional interpretation. Questions of liberty affect both our daily lives and our country's values, from what we can say to whom we can marry, how society views us to how we determine our leaders. It is Americans' great privilege that we live under a Constitution that both protects our liberty and allows us to debate what that liberty should be.

The central features of constitutional liberty are freedom and equality, values that are often in tension. One of the Constitution's most important declarations of freedom comes in the First Amendment, which provides that "Congress shall make no law respecting an establishment of religion, or prohibiting the free exercise thereof; or abridging the freedom of speech, or of the press; or the right of the people peaceably to assemble, and to petition the Government for a redress of grievances." And one of its most important declarations of equality comes in the Fourteenth Amendment, which reads in part, "no State shall . . . deny to any person within its jurisdiction the equal protection of the laws." These Penguin Liberty volumes look in depth at these conceptions of liberty, while also exploring what mechanisms the Constitution has to protect its guarantees of liberty.

Freedom of speech provides a good place to begin to explore the Constitution's idea of liberty. It is a value that enables both the protection of liberty and the right of citizens to debate its meaning. Textually, the constitutional guarantee that Congress cannot limit free speech might read as though it is absolute. Yet for much of U.S. history, free speech protections were minimal. In 1798, President John Adams signed the Sedition Act, essentially making it a crime to criticize the president or the U.S. government. During the Civil War, President Abraham Lincoln had some dissidents and newspapers silenced. In 1919, a moment came that seemed to protect free speech, when Justice Oliver Wendell Holmes Jr. wrote in

Schenck v. United States that speech could be limited only when it posed a "clear and present danger." But, in fact, this ruling did little to protect free speech, as the Court repeatedly interpreted danger so broadly that minority viewpoints, especially leftist viewpoints, were often seen as imprisonable.

Today, however, U.S. free speech protections are the most expansive in the world. All viewpoints are allowed to be expressed, except for direct threats and incitements to violence. Even many forms of hate speech and opinions attacking democracy itself—types of speech that would be illegal in other countries—are generally permitted here, in the name of free expression. The Court's governing standard is annunciated in *Brandenburg v. Ohio*, which protects vast amounts of speech as long as that speech does not incite "imminent lawless action." How did we get from the Sedition Act to here?

Two thinkers have played an outsize role: John Stuart Mill and Alexander Meiklejohn. Mill's 1859 classic *On Liberty* is an ode to the idea that both liberty and truth will thrive in an open exchange of ideas, where all opinions are allowed to be challenged. In this "marketplace of ideas," as Mill's idea has often come to be called, the truth stays vibrant instead of decaying or descending into dogma. Mill's idea explains the virtue of free speech and the importance of a book series about liberty: Challenging accepted ideas about what liberty is helps bring the best ideas to light. Meiklejohn's theory focuses more on the connection between free speech and democracy. To him, the value of free speech is not just for the speakers, but just as much for the listeners. In a democracy, only when citizens hear all ideas can they come to informed conclusions about how society should be governed. And only informed citizens can fully exercise other democratic rights besides speech, like the right to vote. Meiklejohn's insistence that democratic citizens need a broad exposure to ideas of liberty inspires this series.

Freedom of religion is another central constitutional value that allows citizens the liberty to be who they are and believe what they wish. It is enshrined in the First Amendment, where the Establishment Clause prevents government endorsement of a religion and the Free Exercise Clause gives citizens the freedom to practice their religion. Though these two religion clauses are widely embraced now, they were radically new at the time of the founding. Among the first European settlers in America were the Puritans, members of a group of English Protestants who were persecuted for their religion in their native Britain. But colonial America did not immediately and totally embrace religious toleration. The Church of England still held great sway in the South during the colonial era, and many states had official religions—even after the Constitution forbade a national religion. At the time the Constitution was ratified, secular government was a rarity.

But religious tolerance was eventually enshrined into the U.S. Constitution, thanks in large part to the influence of two thinkers. British philosopher John Locke opposed systems of theocracy. He saw how government-imposed religious beliefs stifled the freedom of minority believers and imposed religious dogma on unwilling societies. In the United States, James Madison built on Locke's ideas when he drafted the First Amendment. The Free Exercise Clause protected the personal freedom to worship, acknowledging the importance of religious practice among Americans. But on Madison's understanding, the Establishment Clause ensured against theocratic imposition of religion by government. Doing so respected the equality of citizens by refusing to allow the government to favor some people's religious beliefs over others.

A more explicit defense of equality comes from the Equal Protection Clause of the Fourteenth Amendment. But as our volume on the Supreme Court shows, the Constitution has not always been interpreted to promote equality. Before the Civil

War, African Americans had few if any formal rights. Millions of African American people were enslaved, and so-called congressional compromises maintained racial subordination long after the importation of slaves was banned in 1808. A burgeoning abolitionist movement gained moral momentum in the North, though the institution of slavery persisted. Liberty was a myth for enslaved people, who were unable to move freely, form organizations, earn wages, or participate in politics.

Still, the Supreme Court, the supposed protector of liberty, for decades failed to guarantee it for African Americans. And in its most notorious ruling it revealed the deep-seated prejudices that had helped to perpetuate slavery. Chief Justice Roger Taney wrote in the 1857 decision in *Dred Scott v. Sandford* that African Americans were not citizens of the United States and "had no rights which the white man was bound to respect." Taney's words were one spark for the Civil War, which, once won by the Union, led to the passage of the Thirteenth, Fourteenth, and Fifteenth Amendments. By ending slavery, granting citizenship and mandating equal legal protection, and outlawing racial discrimination in voting, these Reconstruction Amendments sought to reverse Taney's heinous opinion and provide a platform for advancing real equality.

History unfortunately shows us, however, that legal equality did not translate into real equality for African Americans. Soon after Reconstruction, the Court eviscerated the Fourteenth Amendment's scope, then ruled in 1896 in *Plessy v. Ferguson* that racial segregation was constitutional if the separate facilities were deemed equal. This paved the way for the legally sanctioned institution of Jim Crow segregation, which relegated blacks to second-class citizenship, denying them meaningful social, legal, and political equality. Finally, facing immense pressure from civil rights advocates including W. E. B. Du Bois and A. Philip Randolph, as well as the powerful legal reasoning of NAACP lawyer Thurgood Marshall, the Court gave the Equal Protection Clause teeth, culminating in the landmark 1954 *Brown v. Board of Education* decision, which declared that in public education, separate is "inherently unequal." Even after that newfound defense of constitutional equality, however, racial inequality has persisted, with the Court and country debating the meaning of liberty and equal protection in issues as varied as affirmative action and racial gerrymandering.

While the Fourteenth Amendment was originally passed with a specific intention to end racial discrimination, its language is general: "No State shall . . . deny to any person within its jurisdiction the equal protection of the laws." Over time, that generality has allowed civil rights advocates to expand the meaning of equality to include other groups facing discrimination. One significant example is the fight for gender equality.

Women had been left out of the Constitution; masculine pronouns pepper the original document, and women are not mentioned." In an 1807 letter to Albert Gallatin, Thomas Jefferson—the person who had penned the Declaration of Independence—wrote that "the appointment of a woman to office is an innovation for which the public is not prepared, nor am I." Liberty was a myth for many women, who were supposed to do little outside the home, had limited rights to property, were often made to be financially dependent on their husbands, and faced immense barriers to political participation.

Nevertheless, women refused to be shut out of politics. Many were influential in the burgeoning temperance and abolition movements of the nineteenth century. In 1848, Elizabeth Cady Stanton wrote the Declaration of Sentiments, amending the Declaration of Independence to include women. Still, suffragists were left out when the Fifteenth Amendment banned voting discrimination based on race—but not on gender. Only after Alice Paul and others led massive protests would the freedom to vote be constitutionally guaranteed for women through the Nineteenth Amendment.

Voting secured one key democratic liberty, but women were still denied the full protection of legal equality. They faced discrimination in the workplace, laws based on sexist stereotypes, and a lack of reproductive autonomy. That's where our volume on Supreme Court justice Ruth Bader Ginsburg begins. Now a feminist icon from her opinions on the Court, Justice Ginsburg earlier served as a litigator with the ACLU, leading their Women's Rights Project, where she helped to convince the Court to consider gender as a protected class under the Fourteenth Amendment. As a justice, she continued her pioneering work to deliver real gender equality, knowing that women would never enjoy the full scope of constitutional liberty unless they held the same legal status as men.

Ginsburg's work underscores how the meaning of constitutional liberty has expanded over time. While the Declaration of Independence did explicitly reference equality, the Bill of Rights did not. Then, with the Reconstruction Amendments, especially the Equal Protection Clause, the Constitution was imbued with a new commitment to equality. Now the document affirmed that democratic societies must protect both negative liberties for citizens to act freely and positive liberties for all to be treated as equal democratic citizens. Never has this tension between freedom and equality been perfectly resolved, but the story of our Constitution is that it has often inspired progress toward realizing liberty for more Americans.

Progress has been possible not just because of an abstract constitutional commitment to liberty, but also due to formal mechanisms that help us to guarantee it. Impeachment is the Constitution's most famous—and most explosive—way to do so. With the abuses of monarchy in mind, the framers needed a way to thwart tyranny and limit concentrated power. Borrowing in language and spirit from the British, who created a system of impeachment to check the power of the king, they wrote this clause into the Constitution: "The President . . . shall be removed from Office on Impeachment for, and Conviction of, Treason, Bribery, or other high Crimes and Misdemeanors."

Early drafts suggested grounds for impeachment should be just "treason or bribery." But George Mason and other delegates objected, wanting impeachable offenses to include broader abuses of power, not just criminal actions. Though Mason's original suggestion of "maladministration" was rejected, the ultimate language of "high Crimes and Misdemeanors" made it possible to pursue impeachment against leaders who threatened the Constitution's deeper values. Impeachment would stand as the ultimate check on officials who have overstepped their constitutional authority.

The House has formally impeached twenty officials throughout American history, and many more have faced some kind of impeachment inquiry. Most of those accused have been federal judges. Just four impeachment proceedings have reached the presidency, the highest echelon of American government. Andrew Johnson, Bill Clinton, and Donald Trump have been formally impeached, though none were removed from office. Richard Nixon resigned after the House Judiciary Committee voted to impeach, before the full House vote could take place. Most of these impeachment proceedings had a background context in which a president was thought to have violated fundamental constitutional liberties—even if that violation was not always the primary component of the impeachment hearings themselves.

For Johnson, although his impeachment focused on the Tenure of Office Act, an underlying issue was his violation of the liberty of newly freed African Americans to live in society as equals. For Nixon, the impeachment inquiry focused on the Watergate break-in and cover-up, which threatened the liberty of voters to have fair elections and a criminally accountable president. For Clinton, who was accused of perjury and obstruction of justice related to a sexual affair with a White House intern, critics argued that his flouting of criminal laws threatened the standard of equal justice under law—a standard necessary for democratic self-government. For Trump, the impeachment articles accused him of soliciting foreign interference as an abuse of power—threatening the liberty of voters to have fair elections. Often, legalistic questions of criminal wrongdoing dominated these impeachment discussions, but concerns about violations of constitutional liberty were always present in the background.

While impeachment is an important remedy for presidential abuse of liberty, liberty lives best when it is respected before crises arise. To do so requires that liberty not be relegated to an idea just for the purview of courts; rather, citizens and officials should engage in discussions about the meaning of liberty, reaffirming its centrality in everyday life.

By few people are those discussions better modeled than by the example of the now hip-hop famous Alexander Hamilton, a founding father and the nation's first secretary of the treasury. Hamilton was a prolific writer, and in our volumes we'll see him square off against other founders in debates on many major challenges facing the early republic. Against Samuel Seabury, Hamilton rejected the British colonial system and said liberty must come through independence. Against Thomas Jefferson (in an argument now immortalized as a Broadway rap battle), Hamilton advocated for a national bank, believing that a modern, industrial economy was needed to grow the nation. Against James Madison, he pushed for stronger foreign policy powers for the president.

The specifics of Hamilton's debates matter. His ideas shaped American notions of government power, from self-determination to economic growth to international engagement. He was instrumental in ratifying the very Constitution that still grants us our liberties today. But just as important as *what* he argued for was *how* he argued for it. Hamilton thought deeply about what liberty meant to him, and engaged in thoughtful, reasoned discussions with people he disagreed with. He cared both for his own freedoms and for the country's welfare at large.

My goal is for readers of these Penguin Liberty volumes to emulate Hamilton's passion for defending his ideas—even, or especially, if they disagree with him on what liberty means. Everyday citizens are the most important readers of this series— and the most important Americans in the struggle to protect and expand constitutional liberty. Without pressure from the citizenry to uphold constitutional ideals, elected leaders can too easily scrap them. Without citizens vigorously examining the meaning of liberty, its power could be lost. Left untended, the flames of liberty could quietly burn out.

The writings in these Penguin Liberty volumes are intended to give citizens the tools to contest and explore the meaning of liberty so it may be kept alive. None of the selections are simple enough to be summed up in tweets or dismissed with quick insults. They are reasoned, thoughtful attempts to defend constitutional ideals of liberty—or warnings about what can happen when those liberties are disregarded. The Constitution's guarantees of liberty have always been aspirations, not realized accomplishments. Yet if these volumes and other constitutional writings inspire us to bring discussions to dinner tables, classrooms, and workplaces across the country, they will be contributing to making those high ideals more real.

COREY BRETTSCHNEIDER

Introduction

Liberty courses through the veins of the U.S. Constitution. Freedom of speech is protected in the First Amendment, freedom from discrimination in the Fourteenth, and freedom from many forms of arbitrary government intervention in much of the Bill of Rights. However, these statements of liberty are theoretical, abstract; they mean little if they are unenforceable, mere words on paper. To secure liberty governments must be set up to protect it. Often this can be done by empowering legislatures to pass laws giving defined legal force to abstract principles, such as the Thirteenth Amendment's Section 2: "The Congress shall have power to enforce this article by appropriate legislation."

But sometimes the biggest threat to liberty comes not from citizens defying laws, but from public officials abusing their offices, violating the rights of the people they are supposed to serve. The Framers were all too aware of how an all-powerful leader could become a tyrant and trample on freedom; their revolution was fought to create an alternative to monarchy. So they built into the Constitution a safeguard, the ultimate option to depose a leader who threatened the country or abused their office: impeachment.

Article II, Section 4 reads: "The President, Vice President, and all civil Officers of the United States, shall be removed from Office on Impeachment for, and Conviction of, Treason, Bribery, or other high Crimes and Misdemeanors." Other parts of the Constitution clarify the details. A majority vote in the House is necessary to impeach an official, which sets up a trial in the Senate—presided over by the Chief Justice of the Supreme Court—where a two-thirds vote is needed for conviction. Punishment for impeachment is restricted to removal from office, with criminal indictment a separate process.

Despite these constitutional instructions, impeachment is not well understood by the public. The phrase "high Crimes and Misdemeanors," along with words like "tried" and "convicted," make impeachment sound like a process of criminal law, but it's not. There is no such legal category as a "high crime." Rather, the Founders adopted the phrase from the British, who codified their idea of impeachment centuries earlier and used "high crimes and misdemeanors" as part of their standard. They used impeachment to remove corrupt ministers of the king, giving Parliament a way to protect the people's rights, even when officials had not committed a formal crime. Impeachment was even most famously used against King Charles I, who was formally impeached before ultimately being executed for his role in fomenting civil war.

At the U.S. Constitutional Convention, many of the Framers wanted to emulate this broad category of impeachment. Early drafts included only treason and bribery as impeachable offenses, but delegates including George Mason worried that including only these terms would too narrowly limit our ability to rein in presidents who abused power in other ways. Though Mason's suggestion of "maladministration" was rejected, perhaps being seen as too broad, the delegates ultimately chose the phrase "high Crimes and Misdemeanors." With this formal langauge chosen, the Framers had created a formal political process for removing our highest officials—

strong enough to peacefully depose presidents while maintaining a stable democracy.

Still, the idea of presidents willingly giving up their powers was not a typical proposition at a time when monarchs ruled much of the world with near-absolute power. So when George Washington took the podium for his second inaugural address, the Constitution still in its infancy, impeachment remained abstract, like many of the Constitution's other liberty protections. Washington, the hero of the country, widely trusted and adored, could have tried to flout the Constitution and amass kingly powers. He did just the opposite.

His 135-word second inaugural demonstrates the restraints of a president committed to protecting citizens' liberties. Washington implores his listeners (both Congress and the country) to subject him to "constitutional punishment" if he fails to abide by his presidential oath to "preserve, protect, and defend" the Constitution. For some violations, he suggests "upbraidings," or criticisms, of the president. For other, larger violations of liberty, the "constitutional punishment" he suggests may mean impeachment.

Washington's idea of constitutional punishment helps us see how impeachment protects the presidency itself. By making clear the presidential office is distinct from its temporary occupants, Washington framed the idea of holding a president accountable not as a partisan move, but as a way to ensure leaders live up to constitutional ideals. Impeachment, a central mechanism for holding presidents to account, protects liberty by nonviolently removing those who threaten liberty from within the government itself.

That's impeachment in its ideal form, and that's why it is a core component of this series about liberty. But in this volume, we'll go beyond just what impeachment is in theory. We'll explore whether impeachment really has been used to protect liberty—or whether it has actually threatened liberty.

Our three case studies—Andrew Johnson, Bill Clinton, and Richard Nixon (who resigned before facing his inevitable impeachment)—represent the only three presidents to face formal impeachment inquiries before the twenty-first century, when Donald Trump was impeached by the House and became the fourth. By providing the key documents surrounding each impeachment, we put readers in the position of a senator, asking you to judge for yourself whether each president's conduct justified impeachment and removal.

We begin with Andrew Johnson, the nation's seventeenth president, and the first to be impeached when the House voted 126 to 47 to impeach him on February 24, 1868. On the surface, his case was about a relatively narrow legal dispute. Johnson had tried to fire Edwin Stanton, his secretary of war, a holdover from the Abraham Lincoln administration. However, under the Tenure of Office Act enacted in 1867, the president could not remove Senate-confirmed executive branch officials without the consent of the Senate. Based on his disregard of this law, Republicans in Congress alleged Johnson did not faithfully execute the law as his oath demanded. Nine of the eleven articles of impeachment directly concerned the Stanton affair. Even the highly publicized Senate trial focused heavily on the legal minutiae of Stanton's firing.

But the Tenure of Office controversy was not the only reason Congress wanted Johnson removed from office. Underlying the Republicans' zeal for impeachment was their hatred of Johnson for rejecting their civil rights bills and undermining Reconstruction policies in the South designed to protect freed African Americans after the Civil War. For some, firing Stanton, inappropriate and perhaps illegal as it was, was just one more abstract in a long-standing battle with what many in Congress saw as an obstructionist president.

Congress's decision to bury of the deeper, liberty-protecting reasons for impeachment set a troubling precedent. Johnson's constitutional abuses were numerous, his abject refusal to provide for the welfare of formerly enslaved citizens or grant them meaningful freedom a clear violation of the Constitution's values. Impeaching him just for firing Stanton sent the message that only legal violations were grounds for impeachment; Congress treated "high crimes and misdemeanors" as a legal standard, when it was supposed to encompass broader abuses of the office. Impeaching Johnson simply for removing a cabinet secretary he did not even appoint himself seemed partisan and excessive to many onlookers.

This failure has allowed critics, then and now, to dismiss the Johnson impeachment as an unjust and partisan affair. The Senate was unconvinced of Johnson's wrongdoing, failing to reach the two-thirds majority needed for conviction, though by a margin of just one vote. John F. Kennedy's famous book *Profiles in Courage* even lauded Kansas senator Edmund Ross for breaking with the Republican Party to cast the decisive not guilty vote.

These critics miss the essential moral point of the impeachment, one best stated by Frederick Douglass, a leading African American orator of his day and a fierce critic of Johnson. In an 1866 essay for *The Atlantic*, Douglass called Johnson "treacherous" (not "treasonous," as the legalistic constitutional term would be), and accused Johnson of violating his oath by undermining the Constitution's true antislavery and pro–racial equality values. Though Douglass did not in this essay explicitly call for impeachment, his argument suggests that Johnson's failure to advance racial equality violated his oath of office. Another Douglass speech confirms the point: Impeachment of Johnson "will mean the Negros' right to vote, and mean that the fair South shall no longer be governed by the Regulators and the Ku Klux Klan."

Douglass did not win the day. Only some officials, led by Senator Charles Sumner and Representative John Bingham, moralized the case against Johnson during the trial and even still only did so intermittently. But Douglass's insistence on prioritizing the Constitution's deeper values when considering whether presidents have upheld their oaths of office should act as a clarion call for evaluating future impeachments.

More than a century passed before another president faced formal impeachment proceedings. The year was 1972, the president Richard Milhous Nixon. In Washington D.C. on June 17, five men burgled the Democratic National Committee headquarters at the Watergate Complex. *Washington Post* journalists Carl Bernstein and Bob Woodward soon discovered that the burglars were connected to Nixon's Committee to Re-elect the President—known memorably as CREEP.

Public pressure grew to uncover who was involved in the Watergate break-in. In May 1973, former solicitor general Archibald Cox was appointed as a special prosecutor to investigate the Watergate affair. In July, in the course of the Senate Watergate investigation, a Nixon staffer revealed that Nixon had installed a device in the Oval Office on which he secretly recorded tapes of his conversations. But when Cox and Congress demanded that Nixon turn over the tapes, he refused. Incensed by Cox's investigation, he ordered his attorney general Elliot Richardson on October 20 to fire Cox. Richardson refused and resigned. Next in line was William Ruckelshaus, who also refused. Nixon said he fired him, though Ruckelshaus said he resigned. Ultimately, Solicitor General Robert Bork carried out Cox's firing. The event was called the Saturday Night Massacre.

Soon after, the House began an impeachment inquiry, spurred by Nixon's blatantly self-serving abuse of the firing power. As the impeachment process unfolded, so did a legal one. After the firings, public and political outcry pressured Nixon to appoint a new special prosecutor, Leon Jaworski, who as part of an ongoing trial involving Nixon's aides and

Watergate, subpoenaed the president for the secret tapes. Nixon again refused, citing executive privilege. The case soon went to the Supreme Court. Did the president have to turn over the tapes? Was the president immune from criminal indictment?

The indictment debate went all the way back to the Framers. Article I doesn't resolve the question, stating that those impeached will "nevertheless be liable and subject to Indictment," while not clarifying whether that indictment can only happen after impeachment and removal from office or whether a sitting president can be indicted." Alexander Hamilton believed that impeachment must happen first, and only then would presidents be subject to the criminal law. James Wilson, a delegate from Pennsylvania, argued that indictment and impeachment were separate questions, and a president must be indictable while in office to hold him accountable like all other citizens. The constitutional language was left inconclusive.

A week before the Saturday Night Massacre, Nixon's Office of Legal Counsel essentially took Hamilton's side, producing a memo arguing that the president was immune from criminal indictment because of the burdens of his office and the dignity of the presidency. At oral argument in a case at the D.C. District Court in 1974 while discussing the Jaworski subpoenas, Nixon's lawyers followed the same course, comparing Nixon's power to that of a monarch. Jaworski emphatically disagreed. His team wrote a memo making clear that a president must be indictable and his wrongdoing made public, else he step beyond the law.

Jaworski won the legal battle. The Supreme Court ultimately ruled in *United States v. Nixon* that Nixon must comply with the criminal subpoenas and hand over the tapes; The Court said Nixon's claim of absolute executive privilege "cannot prevail over the fundamental demands of due process of law in the fair administration of criminal justice." No decision was reached on the broader question whether a president can be criminally indicted.

Apart from the struggle going on in the courts, impeachment was engulfing Congress. Aides testified to Nixon's knowledge of and role in the break-in and cover-up. Former White House counsel John Dean blew the impeachment investigation wide open, testifying in exquisite detail about Nixon's firsthand efforts to thwart investigations and pay off people who could reveal what they had done. And once the existence of the tapes became clear, momentum for impeachment grew and pressure on Nixon to resign mounted.

Ultimately the Judiciary Committee passed three articles of impeachment, addressing Nixon's obstruction of justice, interference with investigations, and disregard of subpoenas. The committee's Democrats were united for impeachment. In her powerful speech, Representative Barbara Jordan declared: "I am not going to sit here and be an idle spectator to the diminution, the subversion, the destruction, of the Constitution."

But impeachment needed bipartisan support, both to secure the two-thirds majority needed for a Senate conviction and for public viability. Early on in the Watergate affair, Republicans toed the party line by opposing impeachment, buoyed by polling suggesting only 19 percent of Americans favored it. By the time the testimony had concluded and most of the tapes had been released, however, Republican defectors emerged, bolstered by new polling showing a near-majority of Americans were for impeachment. One such defector, Representative Robert McClory, declared that the impeachment must be a "guide for future presidents" on the perils of violating the Constitution.

Ultimately, all twenty-one Democrats voted for the first two articles of impeachment, and six Republicans joined them on each vote, a bipartisan statement that showed Nixon's abuses transcended party politics. Yet to get the sixty-seven votes needed for Senate conviction, even more Republicans would need to vote against their party's president. Their impetus came when Nixon was forced to hand over the last of the secret tapes, which revealed damning evidence that turned even Nixon's staunchest defenders against him. Delivering the final blow, Republican senator Barry Goldwater led a delegation to the White House telling Nixon he might have only four supporters left in the Senate.

Facing this immense political and public pressure, Nixon resigned the presidency. He remains the first and only president to have done so. His resignation allowed him to avoid the humiliation of a House and Senate impeachment vote that would likely have been an emphatic rejection of his presidency. He even was pardoned of all criminal wrongdoing by his successor, President Gerald Ford. But the Nixon impeachment affair sent a clear message to the country that the constitutional commitments of Congress could, in extreme circumstances, outweigh the pressures of partisanship and bring the country together in defense of the rule of law.

Two decades later, the third presidential impeachment began. Like Johnson's, the process was dogged from the start by accusations of partisanship. Like Nixon's, the president was charged with obstruction of justice. But William Jefferson Clinton's situation raised unique questions about the outer limits of impeachment's scope.

Clinton's presidency was marked by scandal as soon as it began in 1992. By 1994, Ken Starr had been appointed as the new independent counsel, tasked with investigating Clinton's role in Whitewater (a real estate financing controversy), and later the apparent suicide of White House aide Vince Foster. The Foster case led nowhere, and Whitewater did not directly implicate Clinton in wrongdoing. But Starr, protected from firing by the independent counsel law, was authorized by the attorney general to continue to expand his investigations, and ultimately unearthed the linchpin to impeachment: President Clinton had been having a sexual affair with twenty-two-year-old White House intern Monica Lewinsky.

On its own Clinton's affair with Lewinsky poses a difficult question: Is immoral conduct, outside the official capacity of being president, impeachable? But that was not what Congress focused on. What they did focus on were the allegations that Clinton, in trying to cover up the affair, committed additional offenses, including lying under oath about his relationship with Lewinsky and instructing his personal secretary to hide damaging materials. Starr's final report concluded that Clinton had committed perjury and obstruction of justice.

But Starr did not pursue a criminal indictment. A memo in 1998 written by a law professor Starr commissioned argued cogently against the Nixon-era memo saying that a president could not be indicted. The 1998 memo instead concluded that the president could be indicted; presidents are not above the law and must face the same procedures as other citizens. Starr declined to take this route of prosecution. Instead, he turned his information over to Congress, putting the next step in their hands.

Congress leapt at the opportunity. The Judiciary Committee produced four articles of impeachment, focused on perjury, obstruction of justice, witness manipulation, and interference with impeachment investigators, in some ways echoing the articles of impeachment against Nixon. The perjury and obstruction charges passed the full House on a party-line vote. Clinton became the second president to be formally impeached.

At the Senate trial, Clinton's lawyers argued the impeachment was partisan. They said that unless there was evidence "beyond a reasonable doubt" that Clinton committed an underlying crime—which they believed there was not—the will of the voters should not be overturned. The public seemed to buy that argument. Clinton was acquitted in the Senate, again on a party-line vote. When Senator Dianne Feinstein, a Democrat, called for a censure resolution to say that Clinton's actions, while not impeachable, were wrong, she was rebuffed. Clinton's popularity numbers did not even take a dent during his impeachment.

Clinton himself got off the hook. But his impeachment undermined the hope that future presidents could be subject to an objective, bipartisan, respected impeachment process. Under Nixon, the bipartisan consensus that his actions were wrong lent impeachment legitimacy and built public support for a constitutional standard of removal. Under Clinton, the impeachment was vitriolic, with partisan conflict central. People saw impeachment as a legal process bastardized by politics, instead of as a political process tempered by constitutional values, as the Framers intended. The Clinton defenders' technical legal arguments diminished impeachment's broader political purpose.

Where does that leave us with impeachment today? Can it still be the tool the Framers envisioned to thwart tyranny and protect constitutional liberty? Or has it become outdated, a political process too subject to partisanship and power struggles?

The impeachment of a fourth president, Donald Trump, reinforces that what may seem like abstract questions around the meaning of impeachment still have urgency in the lives of Americans. And for some people, the failure of the Senate to ever reach the two-thirds vote necessary for convicting and removing a president suggests the process is ineffective. Yet if impeachment is not the way to stop a rogue president, we need to figure out what is. In this volume readers will get a tour through the history of presidential impeachment, inspiring us to think about what impeachment is for and how it should work today. The concern at the Founding that the president would become an unaccountable tyrant can only be addressed if there is a way to hold such a high official to account. Impeachment was meant to be that process. My hope is that in studying these texts, readers will be inspired to make that ideal real.

Corey Brettschneider

A Note on the Text

All the works in this selection are excerpted, except the "Second Inaugural Address" of George Washington. Spelling and punctuation are kept as in the original. Footnotes have been eliminated from the text without marking. All works are in the public domain, and can be found within the "Unabridged Source Materials" section in this book.

Part I

ORIGINS OF IMPEACHMENT

U.S. Constitution

The process of impeachment is outlined in just a few phrases in the U.S. Constitution. Article I grants Congress the power to try impeachment, lays out the standard for convicting a president, explains how the trial works, and establishes the punishment. Article II then explains what offenses merit removal of a president: "Treason, Bribery, or other high Crimes and Misdemeanors." In these few short words, the Constitution created a peaceful process for removing the country's most powerful official—unheard of in the era of monarchs during which it was written.

Article I, Section 2, Clause 5: The House of Representatives shall chuse their Speaker and other officers; and shall have the sole Power of Impeachment.

Article I, Section 3, Clause 6: The Senate shall have the sole Power to try all Impeachments. When sitting for that Purpose, they shall be on Oath or Affirmation. When the President of the United States is tried, the Chief Justice shall preside: And no Person shall be convicted without the Concurrence of two thirds of the Members present.

Article I, Section 3, Clause 7: Judgment in Cases of impeachment shall not extend further than to removal from Office, and disqualification to hold and enjoy any Office of honor, Trust or Profit under the United States: but the Party convicted shall nevertheless be liable and subject to Indictment, Trial, Judgment and Punishment, according to Law.

Article II, Section 2, Clause 1: The President shall . . . have Power to grant Reprieves and Pardons for Offences against the United States, except in Cases of Impeachment.

Article II, Section 4: The President, Vice President and all civil Officers of the United States, shall be removed from Office on Impeachment for, and Conviction of, Treason, Bribery, or other high Crimes and Misdemeanors.

Article III, Section 2, Clause 3: The Trial of all Crimes, except in Cases of Impeachment, shall be by Jury . . .

Notes from the Debates of the Constitutional Convention (July 20, 1787)

The Constitution's adopted form was the product of robust debate from the Constitutional Convention, held in Philadelphia in 1787. Among many other topics, the delegates discussed impeachment, debating how best to hold the newly created presidency accountable. James Madison's notes from the debates, excerpted here, capture a wide range of views on the topic, from Charles Pinkney's belief that there should be no impeachment, to Madison's own belief that the people, supreme in a democracy, must retain the right to remove their leaders.

On question on . . . "to be removeable on impeachment and conviction for malpractice or neglect of duty."

Mr. PINKNEY & Mr. Govr. MORRIS moved to strike out this part of the Resolution. Mr. P. observd. he ought not to be impeachable whilst in office.

Mr. DAVIE. If he be not impeachable whilst in office, he will spare no efforts or means whatever to get himself re-elected. He considered this as an essential security for the good behaviour of the Executive. . . .

Mr. Govr. MORRIS. He can do no criminal act without Co-adjutors who may be punished. In case he should be re-elected, that will be sufficient proof of his innocence. Besides who is to impeach? Is the impeachment to suspend his functions. If it is not the mischief will go on. If it is the impeachment will be nearly equivalent to a displacement, and will render the Executive dependent on those who are to impeach.

Col. MASON. No point is of more importance than that the right of impeachment should be continued. Shall any man be above Justice? Above all shall that man be above it, who can commit the most extensive injustice? When great crimes were committed he was for punishing the principal as well as the Coadjutors. . . .

Docr. FRANKLIN was for retaining the clause as favorable to the Executive. History furnishes one example only of a first Magistrate being formally brought to public Justice. Every body cried out agst. this as unconstitutional. What was the practice before this in cases where the chief Magistrate rendered himself obnoxious? Why recourse was had to assassination in wch. he was not only deprived of his life but of the opportunity of vindicating his character. It wd.. be the best way therefore to provide in the Constitution for the regular punishment of the Executive where his misconduct should deserve it, and for his honorable acquittal when he should be unjustly accused.

Mr. Govr. MORRIS admits corruption & some few other offences to be such as ought to be impeachable; but thought the cases ought to be enumerated & defined.

Mr. MADISON thought it indispensable that some provision should be made for defending the Community agst. the incapacity, negligence or perfidy of the chief Magistrate. . . . He might lose his capacity after his appointment. He might pervert his administration into a scheme of peculation or oppression. He might betray his trust to foreign powers. The case of the Executive Magistracy was very distinguishable, from that of the Legislature or of any other public body, holding offices of limited duration. . . . In the case of the Executive Magistracy which was to be administered by a single man, loss of capacity or corruption was more within the compass of probable events, and either of them might be fatal to the Republic.

Mr. PINKNEY did not see the necessity of impeachments. He was sure they ought not to issue from the Legislature who would in that case hold them as a rod over the Executive and by that means effectually destroy his independence. His revisionary power in particular would be rendered altogether insignificant.

Mr. GERRY urged the necessity of impeachments. A good magistrate will not fear them. A bad one ought to be kept in fear of them. He hoped the maxim would never be adopted here that the chief magistrate could do no wrong. . . .

Mr. RANDOLPH. The propriety of impeachments was a favorite principle with him. Guilt wherever found ought to be punished. The Executive will have great opportunitys of abusing his power; particularly in time of war when the military force, and in some respects the public money will be in his hands. Should no regular punishment be provided, it will be irregularly inflicted by tumults & insurrections. . . .

Mr. WILSON observed that if the idea were to be pursued, the Senators who are to hold their places during the same term with the Executive, ought to be subject to impeachment & removal.

Mr. PINKNEY apprehended that some gentlemen reasoned on a supposition that the Executive was to have powers which would not be committed to him: He presumed that his powers would be so circumscribed as to render impeachments unnecessary.

Mr. Govr. MORRIS . . . was now sensible of the necessity of impeachments. . . . Our Executive . . . may be bribed by a greater interest to betray his trust; and no one would say that we ought to expose ourselves to the danger of seeing the first Magistrate in foreign pay, without being able to guard agst. it by displacing him. . . . The Executive ought therefore to be impeachable for treachery; Corrupting his electors, and incapacity were other causes of impeachment. For the latter he should be punished not as a man, but as an officer, and punished only by degradation from his office. This Magistrate is not the King but the prime-Minister. The people are the King. When we make him amenable to Justice however we should take care to provide some mode that will not make him dependent on the Legislature.

"The Federalist No. 65," by Alexander Hamilton (March 7, 1788)

The Federalist written by Alexander Hamilton, James Madison, and John Jay, was a series of essays, published under the pseudonym Publius, advocating for the ratification of the Constitution. The essays are now widely regarded as an authoritative source on the meaning of the Constitution and the views of some of its most important Framers. Here, in essay number 65, Hamilton defends the idea that Congress is better suited than the Court to remove the president, since impeachment is rightly seen as addressing political offenses—not legal ones.

A well-constituted court for the trial of impeachments is an object not more to be desired than difficult to be obtained in a government wholly elective. The subjects of its jurisdiction are those offenses which proceed from the misconduct of public men, or, in other words, from the abuse or violation of some public trust. They are of a nature which may with peculiar propriety be denominated POLITICAL, as they relate chiefly to injuries done immediately to the society itself. The prosecution of them, for this reason, will seldom fail to agitate the passions of the whole community, and to divide it into parties more or less friendly or inimical to the accused. In many cases it will connect itself with the pre-existing factions, and will enlist all their animosities, partialities, influence, and interest on one side or on the other; and in such cases there will always be the greatest danger that the decision will be regulated more by the comparative strength of parties, than by the real demonstrations of innocence or guilt.

The delicacy and magnitude of a trust which so deeply concerns the political reputation and existence of every man engaged in the administration of public affairs, speak for themselves. The difficulty of placing it rightly . . . will as readily be perceived, when it is considered that the most conspicuous characters . . . will . . . be too often the leaders or the tools of the most cunning or the most numerous faction, and on this account, can hardly be expected to possess the requisite neutrality towards those whose conduct may be the subject of scrutiny.

The convention, it appears, thought the Senate the most fit depositary of this important trust. . . . It is not disputed that the power of originating the inquiry, or, in other words, of preferring the impeachment, ought to be lodged in the hands of one branch of the legislative body. . . .

Where else than in the Senate could have been found a tribunal sufficiently dignified, or sufficiently independent? What other body would be likely to feel confidence enough in its own situation, to preserve, unawed and uninfluenced, the necessary impartiality between an individual accused, and the representatives of the people, his accusers?

Could the Supreme Court have been relied upon as answering this description? It is much to be doubted, whether the members of that tribunal would at all times be endowed with so eminent a portion of fortitude, as would be called for in the execution of so difficult a task; and it is still more to be doubted, whether they would possess the degree of credit and authority, which might, on certain occasions, be indispensable towards reconciling the people to a decision that should happen to clash with an accusation brought by their immediate representatives. A deficiency in the first, would be fatal to the accused; in the last, dangerous to the public tranquility. . . . There will be no jury to stand between the judges who are to pronounce the sentence of the law, and the party who is to receive or suffer it. The awful discretion which a court of impeachments must necessarily have, to doom to honor or to infamy the most confidential and the most distinguished characters of the community, forbids the commitment of the trust to a small number of persons.

These considerations seem alone sufficient to authorize a conclusion, that the Supreme Court would have been an improper substitute for the Senate, as a court of impeachments. There remains a further consideration, which will not a little strengthen this conclusion. It is this: The punishment which may be the consequence of conviction upon impeachment, is not to terminate the chastisement of the offender. After having been sentenced to a perpetual ostracism from the esteem and confidence, and honors and emoluments of his country, he will still be liable to prosecution and punishment in the ordinary course of law. Would it be proper that the persons who had disposed of his fame, and his most valuable rights as a citizen in one trial, should, in another trial, for the same offense, be also the disposers of his life and his fortune? . . . By making the same persons judges in both cases, those who might happen to be the objects of prosecution would, in a great measure, be deprived of the double security intended them by a double trial. . . .

Would it have been an improvement of the plan, to have united the Supreme Court with the Senate, in the formation of the court of impeachments? This union would certainly have been attended with several advantages; but would they not have been overbalanced by the signal disadvantage, already stated, arising from the agency of the same judges in the double prosecution to which the offender would be liable? To a certain extent, the benefits of that union will be obtained from making the chief justice of the Supreme Court the president of the court of impeachments, as is proposed to be done in the plan of the convention; while the inconveniences of an entire incorporation of the former into the latter will be substantially avoided. . . .

Would it have been desirable to have composed the court for the trial of impeachments, of persons wholly distinct from the other departments of the government? There are weighty arguments, as well against, as in favor of, such a plan. To some minds it will not appear a trivial objection, that it could tend to increase the complexity of the political machine, and to add a new spring to the government, the utility of which would at best be questionable. But an objection which will not be thought by any unworthy of attention, is this: a court formed upon such a plan, would either be attended with a heavy expense, or might in practice be subject to a variety of casualties and inconveniences. . . .

But though one or the other of the substitutes which have been examined, or some other that might be devised, should be thought preferable to the plan in this respect, reported by the convention, it will not follow that the Constitution ought for this reason to be rejected. If mankind were to resolve to agree in no institution of government, until every part of it had been adjusted to the most exact standard of perfection, society would soon become a general scene of anarchy, and the world a desert. Where is the standard of perfection to be found? Who will undertake to unite the discordant opinions of a whole community, in the same judgment of it; and to prevail upon one conceited projector to renounce his INFALLIBLE criterion for the FALLIBLE criterion of his more

CONCEITED NEIGHBOR? To answer the purpose of the adversaries of the Constitution, they ought to prove, not merely that particular provisions in it are not the best which might have been imagined, but that the plan upon the whole is bad and pernicious.

"Second Inaugural Address," by George Washington (March 4, 1793)

George Washington's second inaugural address is the shortest inaugural in presidential history, at 135 words. Yet in that brief speech, Washington expresses a vital idea: that the president is distinct from the office he or she holds. Washington's call for constitutional punishment for presidents who violate the oath of office can be seen as a reference to presidential impeachment.

Fellow Citizens:

I am again called upon by the voice of my country to execute the functions of its Chief Magistrate. When the occasion proper for it shall arrive, I shall endeavor to express the high sense I entertain of this distinguished honor, and of the confidence which has been reposed in me by the people of united America.

Previous to the execution of any official act of the President the Constitution requires an oath of office. This oath I am now about to take, and in your presence: That if it shall be found during my administration of the Government I have in any instance violated willingly or knowingly the injunctions thereof, I may (besides incurring constitutional punishment) be subject to the upbraidings of all who are now witnesses of the present solemn ceremony.

"Constitutional Grounds for Presidential Impeachment," by the U.S. House of Representatives Committee on the Judiciary (February 22, 1974)

The Constitution's brief discussion of impeachment leaves many of the details imprecisely defined. One result of this imprecision has been persistent confusion about the standard of "high Crimes and Misdemeanors" for an impeachable offense. This government report, written in preparation for the impeachment inquiry into Richard Nixon, traces the history of the phrase, from British Parliamentary practice to the U.S. Constitution. Rightly understood, "high Crimes and Misdemeanors" is not a legal standard, but rather a political one, denoting abuses of an official's office or the public trust.

A. THE ENGLISH PARLIAMENTARY PRACTICE

Alexander Hamilton wrote, in No. 65 of *The Federalist*, that Great Britain had served as "the model from which [impeachment] has been borrowed." Accordingly, its history in England is useful to an understanding of the purpose and scope of the impeachment in the United States.

Parliament developed the impeachment as a means to exercise some measure of control over the King. An impeachment proceeding in England was a direct method of bringing into account the King's ministers and favorites—men who might have otherwise been out of reach. Impeachment, at least in its early history, has been called "the most powerful weapon in the political armoury, short of civil war." It played a continuing role in the struggles between King and Parliament that resulted in the formation of the unwritten English constitution. In this respect impeachment was one of the tools used by English Parliament to create more responsive and responsible government and to redress imbalances when they occurred. . . .

Characteristically, impeachment was used in individual cases to reach offenses, as perceived by Parliament, against the system of government. The charges, variously denominated "treason," "high treason," "misdemeanors," "malversations," and "high Crimes and Misdemeanors," thus included allegations of misconduct as various as the kings (or their ministers) were ingenious in devising means of expanding royal power.

At the time of the Constitutional Convention the phrase "high Crimes and Misdemeanors" had been in use for over 400 years in impeachment proceedings in Parliament. It first appears in 1386 in the impeachment of the King's Chancellor, Michael de le Pole, Earl of Suffolk. . . . de la Pole was charged with breaking a promise he made to the full Parliament . . .

The phrase does not reappear in impeachment proceedings until 1450. In that year articles of impeachment against William de la Pole, Duke of Suffolk (a descendant of Michael), charged him with several acts of high treason, but also with "high Crimes and Misdemeanors," including . . . "advising the King to grant liberties and privileges to certain persons to the hindrance of the due execution of the laws," . . . and "squandering away the public treasure."

. . . During the period from 1620 to 1649 over 100 impeachments were voted by the House of Commons. Some of these impeachments charged high treason, as in the case of Strafford; others charged high crimes and misdemeanors. . . .

The phrase "high Crimes and Misdemeanors" appears in nearly all of the comparatively few impeachments that occurred in the eighteenth century. Many of the charges involved abuse of official power or trust. For example, Edward, Earl of Oxford, was charged in 1701 with "violation of his duty and trust" in that, while a member of the King's privy council, he took advantage of the ready access he had to the King to secure various royal rents and revenues for his own use, thereby greatly diminishing the revenues of the crown and subjecting the people of England to "grievous taxes." . . .

The impeachment of Warren Hastings, first attempted in 1786 and concluded in 1795, is particularly important because [it was] contemporaneous with the American Convention debates. Hastings was the first Governor-General of India. The articles indicate that Hastings was being charged with high crimes and misdemeanors in the form of gross maladministration, corruption in office, and cruelty toward the people of India.

Two points emerge from the 400 years of English parliamentary experience with the phrase "high Crimes and Misdemeanors." First the particular allegations of misconduct alleged damage to the state in such forms as misapplication of funds, abuse of official power, neglect of duty, encroachment on Parliament's prerogatives, corruption, and betrayal of trust. Second, the phrase "high Crimes and Misdemeanors" was confined to parliamentary impeachments; it had no roots in the ordinary criminal law, and the particular allegations of misconduct under that heading were not necessarily limited to common law or statutory derelictions or crimes.

B. THE INTENTION OF THE FRAMERS . . .

1. The Purpose of the Impeachment Remedy

. . . Impeachment had been included in the proposals before the Constitutional Convention from its beginning. A specific provision, making the executive removable from office on impeachment and conviction for "mal-practice or neglect of duty," was unanimously adopted even before it was decided that the executive would be a single person.

The only major debate on the desirability of impeachment occurred when it was moved that the provision for impeachment be dropped, a motion that was defeated by a vote of eight states to two. . . .

2. Adoption of "High Crimes and Misdemeanors"

. . . The draft of the Constitution then before the Convention provided for [the president's] removal upon impeachment and conviction for "treason or bribery." George Mason objected that these grounds were too limited . . .

Mason then moved to add the word "maladministration" to the other two grounds. Maladministration was a term in use in six of the thirteen state constitutions as a ground for impeachment, including Mason's home state of Virginia.

When James Madison objected that "so vague a term will be equivalent to a tenure during pleasure of the Senate," Mason withdrew "maladministration" and substituted "high crimes and misdemeanors agst. the State," which was adopted eight states to three, apparently with no further debate. . . .

. . . Blackstone's *Commentaries on the Laws of England*—a work cited by delegates in other portions of the Convention's deliberations and which Madison later described (in the Virginia ratifying convention) as "a book which is in every man's hand"—included "high misdemeanors" as one term for positive offenses "against the king and government. "The "first and principal" high misdemeanor, according to Blackstone, was "mal-administration of such high officers, as are in public trust and employment," usually punished by the method of parliamentary impeachment."

"High Crimes and Misdemeanors" has traditionally been considered a "term of art," like such other constitutional phrases as "levying war" and "due process." The Supreme Court has held that such phrases must be construed, not according to modern usage, but according to what the farmers meant when they adopted them. Chief Justice Marshall wrote of another such phrase:

It is a technical term. It is used in a very old statute of that country whose language is our language, and whose laws form the substratum of our laws. It is scarcely conceivable that the term was not employed by the framers of our constitution in the sense which had been affixed to it by those from whom we borrowed it.

3. Grounds for Impeachment . . .

Comments in the state ratifying conventions also suggest that those who adopted the Constitution viewed impeachment as a remedy for usurpation or abuse of power or serious breach of trust. Thus, Charles Cotesworth Pinckney of South Carolina stated that the impeachment power of the House reaches "those who behave amiss, or betray their public trust." Edmund Randolph said in the Virginia convention that the President may be impeached if he "misbehaves." He later cited the example of the President's receipt of presents or emoluments from a foreign power in violation of the constitutional prohibition of

Article I, section 9. In the same convention George Mason argued that the President might use his pardoning power to "pardon crimes which were advised by himself" or, before indictment or conviction, "to stop inquiry and prevent detection." James Madison responded:

> [I]f the President be connected, in any suspicious manner, with any person, and there be grounds to believe he will shelter him, the House of Representatives can impeach him; they can remove him if found guilty. . . .

. . . In short, the framers who discussed impeachment in the state ratifying conventions, as well as other delegates who favored the Constitution, implied that it reached offenses against the government, and especially abuses of constitutional duties. The opponents did not argue that the grounds for impeachment had been limited to criminal offenses. . . .

One further piece of contemporary evidence is provided by the *Lectures on Law* delivered by James Wilson of Pennsylvania in 1790 and 1791. Wilson described impeachments in the United States as "confined to political characters, to political crimes and misdemeanors, and to political punishment" And, he said:

> The doctrine of impeachments is of high import in the constitutions of free states. On one hand, the most powerful magistrates should be amenable to the law: on the other hand, elevated characters should not be sacrificed merely on account of their elevation. No one should be secure while he violates the constitution and the laws: every one should be secure while he observes them.

From the comments of the framers and their contemporaries, [and] the remarks of the delegates to the state ratifying conventions . . . it is apparent that the scope of impeachment was not viewed narrowly. It was intended to provide a check on the President through impeachment, but not to make him dependent on the unbridled will of the Congress.

Part II

ANDREW JOHNSON

"Veto Message on Freedmen and Refugee Relief Bureau Legislation," by Andrew Johnson (February 19, 1866)

> *The formal impeachment of Andrew Johnson focused primarily on his firing of Secretary of War Edwin Stanton in alleged violation of the Tenure of Office Act. But many of the Republicans who led the impeachment of Johnson had despised him long before that incident. Republicans sought to advance Reconstruction, the effort to aggressively enforce and establish equal rights for the formerly enslaved African Americans. Johnson, an opponent of Reconstruction, stymied the Republicans at every turn, frustrating their efforts to realize the promise of full citizenship that the Civil War was supposed to bring to African Americans. In this message, Johnson vetoes Congress's proposed Freedmen's Bureau, which would have created a government agency to deliver aid and support to recently freed slaves.*

To the Senate of the United States:

I have examined with care the bill, which originated in the Senate and has been passed by the two Houses of Congress, to amend an act entitled "An act to establish a bureau for the relief of freedmen and refugees," and for other purposes. Having with much regret come to the conclusion that it would not be consistent with the public welfare to give my approval to the measure, I return the bill to the Senate with my objections to its becoming a law. . . .

I share with Congress the strongest desire to secure to the freedmen the full enjoyment of their freedom and property and their entire independence and equality in making contracts for their labor, but the bill before me contains provisions which in my opinion are not warranted by the Constitution and are not well suited to accomplish the end in view.

The bill proposes to establish by authority of Congress military jurisdiction over all parts of the United States containing refugees and freedmen. It . . . expressly extends the existing temporary jurisdiction of the Freedmen's Bureau, with greatly enlarged powers, over those States "in which the ordinary course of judicial proceedings has been interrupted by the rebellion." . . .

The subjects over which this military jurisdiction is to extend in every part of the United States include protection to "all employees, agents, and officers of this bureau in the exercise of the duties imposed" upon them by the bill. In eleven States it is further to extend over all cases affecting freedmen and refugees discriminated against "by local law, custom, or prejudice." In those eleven States the bill subjects any white person who may be charged with depriving a freedman of "any civil rights or immunities belonging to white persons" to imprisonment or fine, or both, without, however, defining the "civil rights and immunities" which are thus to be secured to the freedmen by military law. . . .

The trials having their origin under this bill are to take place without the intervention of a jury and without any fixed rules of law or evidence. The rules on which offenses are to be "heard and determined" by the numerous agents are such rules and regulations as the President, through the War Department, shall prescribe. . . . The punishment will be, not what the law declares, but such as a court-martial may think proper; and from these arbitrary tribunals there lies no appeal, no writ of error to any of the courts in which the Constitution of the United States vests exclusively the judicial power of the country.

. . . I can not reconcile a system of military jurisdiction of this kind with the words of the Constitution. . . . The safeguards which the experience and wisdom of ages taught our fathers to establish as securities for the protection of the innocent, the punishment of the guilty, and the equal administration of justice are to be set aside, and for the sake of a more vigorous interposition in behalf of justice we are to take the risks of the many acts of injustice that would necessarily follow from an almost countless number of agents established in every parish or county in nearly a third of the States of the Union, over whose decisions there is to be no supervision or control by the Federal courts. The power that would be thus placed in the hands of the President is such as in time of peace certainly ought never to be intrusted to any one man. . . .

. . . In time of war it was eminently proper that we should provide for those who were passing suddenly from a condition of bondage to a state of freedom. But this bill proposes to make the Freedmen's Bureau, established by the act of 1865 as one of many great and extraordinary military measures to suppress a formidable rebellion, a permanent branch of the public administration, with its powers greatly enlarged. . . . The institution of slavery, for the military destruction of which the Freedmen's Bureau was called into existence as an auxiliary, has been already effectually and finally abrogated throughout the whole country by an amendment of the Constitution of the United States, and practically its eradication has received the assent and concurrence of most of those States in which it at any time had an existence. . . . If I am correct in these views, there can be no necessity for the enlargement of the powers of the Bureau, for which provision is made in the bill.

The third section of the bill authorizes a general and unlimited grant of support to the destitute and suffering refugees and freedmen, their wives and children. Succeeding sections make provision for the rent or purchase of landed estates for freedmen, and for the erection for their benefit of suitable buildings for asylums and schools, the expenses to be defrayed from the Treasury of the whole people.

The Congress of the United States has never heretofore thought itself empowered to establish asylums beyond the limits of the District of Columbia, except for the benefit of our disabled soldiers and sailors. It has never founded schools for any class of our own people, not even for the orphans of those who have fallen in the defense of the Union, but has left the care of education to the much more competent and efficient control of the States, of communities, of private associations, and of individuals. It has never deemed itself authorized to expend the public money for the rent or purchase of homes for the thousands, not to say millions, of the white race who are honestly toiling from day to day for their subsistence. A system for the support of indigent persons in the United States was never contemplated by the authors of the Constitution; nor can any good reason be advanced why, as a permanent establishment, it should be founded for one class or color of our people more than another. Pending the war many refugees and freedmen received support from the Government, but it was never intended that they should thenceforth be fed, clothed, educated, and sheltered by the United States. The idea on which the slaves were assisted to freedom was that on becoming free they would be a self-sustaining population. Any legislation that shall imply that they are not expected to attain a self-sustaining condition must have a tendency injurious alike to their character and their prospects. . . .

There is still further objection to the bill, on grounds seriously affecting the class of persons to whom it is designed to bring relief. . . .

Undoubtedly the freedman should be protected, but he should be protected by the civil authorities, especially by the exercise of all the constitutional powers of the courts of the United States and of the States. His condition is not so exposed as may at first be imagined. He is in a portion of the country where his labor can not well be spared. Competition for his services from planters, from those who are constructing or repairing railroads, and from capitalists in his vicinage or from other States will enable him to command almost his own terms. He also possesses a perfect right to change his place of abode, and if, therefore, he does not find in one community or State a mode of life suited to his desires or proper remuneration for his labor, he can move to another where that labor is more esteemed and better rewarded. In truth, however, each State, induced by its own wants and interests, will do what is necessary and proper to retain within its borders all the labor that is needed for the development of its resources. . . .

Neither is sufficient consideration given to the ability of the freedmen to protect and take care of themselves. It is no more than justice to them to believe that as they have received their freedom with moderation and forbearance, so they will distinguish themselves by their industry and thrift, and soon show the world that in a condition of freedom they are self-sustaining, capable of selecting their own employment and their own places of abode, of insisting for themselves on a proper remuneration, and of establishing and maintaining their own asylums and schools. It is earnestly hoped that instead of wasting away they will by their own efforts establish for themselves a condition of respectability and prosperity. It is certain that they can attain to that condition only through their own merits and exertions. . . .

In accordance with the Constitution, I return the bill to the Senate, in the earnest hope that a measure involving questions and interests so important to the country will not become a law, unless upon deliberate consideration by the people it shall receive the sanction of an enlightened public judgment.

"Veto Message on Civil Rights Legislation," by Andrew Johnson (March 27, 1866)

Johnson's second major veto (and accompanying message) escalated his tensions with the Republican Congress, contributing to the sentiment that he must be impeached. To make good on the promise of the Thirteenth Amendment, which outlawed chattel slavery nationwide and gave Congress the power to enforce its provisions, Congress passed the Civil Rights Act of 1866. The bill was aimed at "affording reasonable protection to all persons in their constitutional rights of equality before the law, without distinction of race or color." Johnson's veto message on this bill, couched in the language of states' rights and limited government, makes clear his opposition to meaningful civil rights. While he was not an explicit defender of slavery, he was a white supremacist who believed the government should not actively promote the rights of blacks.

To the Senate of the United States:

I regret that the bill, which has passed both Houses of Congress, entitled "An act to protect all persons in the United States in their civil rights and furnish the means of their vindication," contains provisions which I can not approve consistently with my sense of duty to the whole people and my obligations to the Constitution of the United States. I am therefore constrained to return it to the Senate, the House in which it originated, with my objections to its becoming a law.

By the first section of the bill all persons born in the United States and not subject to any foreign power, excluding Indians not taxed, are declared to be citizens of the United States. This provision comprehends the Chinese of the Pacific States, Indians subject to taxation, the people called gypsies, as well as the entire race designated as blacks, people of color. Negroes, mulattoes, and persons of African blood. Every individual of these races born in the United States is by the bill made a citizen of the United States. . . .

. . . If, as is claimed by many, all persons who are native born already are, by virtue of the Constitution, citizens of the United States, the passage of the pending bill can not be necessary to make them such. If, on the other hand, such persons are not citizens, as may be assumed from the proposed legislation to make them such, the grave question presents itself whether, when eleven of the thirty-six States are unrepresented in Congress at the present time, it is sound policy to make our entire colored population and all other excepted classes citizens of the United States.

Four millions of them have just emerged from slavery into freedom. Can it be reasonably supposed that they possess the requisite qualifications to entitle them to all the privileges and immunities of citizens of the United States? . . . Besides, the policy of the Government from its origin to the present time seems to have been that persons who are strangers to and unfamiliar with our institutions and our laws should pass through a certain probation, at the end of which, before attaining the coveted prize, they must give evidence of their fitness to receive and to exercise the rights of citizens as contemplated by the Constitution of the United States. The bill in effect proposes a discrimination against large numbers of intelligent, worthy, and patriotic foreigners, and in favor of the Negro, to whom, after long years of bondage, the avenues to freedom and intelligence have just now been suddenly opened. . . . It is now proposed, by a single legislative enactment, to confer the rights of citizens upon all persons of African descent born within the extended limits of the United States, while persons of foreign birth who make our land their home must undergo a probation of five years, and can only then become citizens . . .

The first section of the bill also contains an enumeration of the rights to be enjoyed by these classes so made citizens "in every State and Territory in the United States." . . . A perfect equality of the white and colored races is attempted to be fixed by Federal law in every State of the Union over the vast field of State jurisdiction covered by these enumerated rights. In no one of these can any State ever exercise any power of discrimination between the different races. . . .

. . . Hitherto every subject embraced in the enumeration of rights contained in this bill has been considered as exclusively belonging to the States. They all relate to the internal police and economy of the respective States. They are matters which in each State concern the domestic condition of its people, varying in each according to its own peculiar circumstances and the safety and well-being of its own citizens. I do not mean to say that upon all these subjects there are not Federal restraints . . . but where can we find a Federal prohibition against the power of any State to discriminate, as do most of them, between aliens and citizens, between artificial persons, called corporations, and natural persons, in the right to hold real estate? If it be granted that Congress can repeal all State laws discriminating between whites and blacks in the subjects covered by this bill, why, it may be asked, may not Congress repeal in the same way all State laws discriminating between the two races on the subjects of suffrage and office? If Congress can declare by law who shall hold lands, who shall testify, who shall have capacity to make a contract in a State, then Congress can by law also declare who, without regard to color or race, shall have the right to sit as a juror or as a judge, to hold any office, and, finally, to vote "in every State and Territory of the United States." . . .

The object of the second section of the bill is to afford discriminating protection to colored persons in the full enjoyment of all the rights secured to them by the preceding section. . . .

This section seems to be designed to apply to some existing or future law of a State or Territory which may conflict with the provisions of the bill now under consideration. It provides for counteracting such forbidden legislation by imposing fine and imprisonment upon the legislators who may pass such conflicting laws, or upon the officers or agents who shall put or attempt to put them into execution.

It means an official offense, not a common crime committed against law upon the persons or property of the black race. . . . Under this section members of State legislatures who should vote for laws conflicting with the provisions of the bill, . . . judges of the State courts who should render judgments in antagonism with its terms, and . . . marshals and sheriffs . . . could be brought before other tribunals and there subjected to fine and imprisonment for the performance of the duties which such State laws might impose.

The legislation thus proposed invades the judicial power of the State. It says to every State court or judge, If you decide that this act is unconstitutional; if you refuse, under the prohibition of a State law, to allow a Negro to testify; if you hold that over such a subject-matter the State law is paramount, and "under color" of a State law refuse the exercise of the right to the Negro, your error of judgment, however conscientious, shall subject you to fine and imprisonment. . . .

. . . The remedy proposed by this section seems to be in this respect not only anomalous, but unconstitutional: for the Constitution guarantees nothing with certainty if it does not insure to the several States the right of making and executing laws in regard to all matters arising within their jurisdiction, subject only to the restriction that in cases of conflict with the Constitution and constitutional laws of the United States the latter should be held to be the supreme law of the land. . . .

It is clear that in States which deny to persons whose rights are secured by the first section of the bill any one of those rights all criminal and civil cases affecting them will, by the provisions of the third section, come under the exclusive cognizance of the Federal tribunals. . . .

. . . Over this vast domain of criminal jurisprudence provided by each State for the protection of its own citizens and for the punishment of all persons who violate its criminal laws, Federal law, whenever it can be made to apply, displaces State law. The question here naturally arises, from what source Congress derives the power to transfer to Federal tribunals certain classes of cases embraced in this section. . . .

It may be assumed that this authority is incident to the power granted to Congress by the Constitution, as recently amended, to enforce, by appropriate legislation, the article declaring that—

Neither slavery nor involuntary servitude, except as a punishment for crime whereof the party shall have been duly convicted, shall exist within the United States or any place subject to their jurisdiction.

It can not, however, be justly claimed that, with a view to the enforcement of this article of the Constitution, there is at present any necessity for the exercise of all the powers which this bill confers. Slavery has been abolished, and at present nowhere exists within the jurisdiction of the United States; nor has there been, nor is it likely there will be, any attempt to revive it by the people or the States. . . .

I do not propose to consider the policy of this bill. To me the details of the bill seem fraught with evil. The white race and the black race of the South have hitherto lived together under the relation of master and slave capital owning labor. Now, suddenly, that relation is changed, and as to ownership capital and labor are divorced. They stand now each master of itself. In this new relation, one being necessary to the other, there will be a new adjustment, which both are deeply interested in making harmonious. Each has equal power in settling the terms, and if left to the laws that regulate capital and labor it is confidently believed that they will satisfactorily work out the problem. Capital, it is true, has more intelligence, but labor is never so ignorant as not to understand its own interests, not to know its own value, and not to see that capital must pay that value.

This bill frustrates this adjustment. It intervenes between capital and labor and attempts to settle questions of political economy through the agency of numerous officials whose interest it will be to foment discord between the two races, for as the breach widens their employment will continue, and when it is closed their occupation will terminate.

In all our history, in all our experience as a people living under Federal and State law, no such system as that contemplated by the details of this bill has ever before been proposed or adopted. They establish for the security of the colored race safeguards which go infinitely beyond any that the General Government has ever provided for the white race. In fact, the distinction of race and color is by the bill made to operate in favor of the colored and against the white race. . . . It is another step, or rather stride, toward centralization and the concentration of all legislative powers in the National Government. The tendency of the bill must be to resuscitate the spirit of rebellion and to arrest the progress of those influences which are more closely drawing around the States the bonds of union and peace.

My lamented predecessor, in his proclamation of the 1st of January, 1863, ordered and declared that all persons held as slaves within certain States and parts of States therein designated were and thenceforward should be free; and further, that the executive government of the United States, including the military and naval authorities thereof, would recognize and maintain the freedom of such persons. This guaranty has been rendered especially obligatory and sacred by the amendment of the Constitution abolishing slavery throughout the United States. I therefore fully recognize the obligation to protect and defend that class of our people whenever and wherever it shall become necessary, and to the full extent compatible with the Constitution of the United States.

Entertaining these sentiments, it only remains for me to say that I will cheerfully cooperate with Congress in any measure that may be necessary for the protection of the civil rights of the freedmen, as well as those of all other classes of persons throughout the United States, by judicial process, under equal and impartial laws, in conformity with the provisions of the Federal Constitution.

"The President at Cleveland: A Characteristic Speech, His Audience Handles Him Roughly," in the *Boston Daily Advertiser* (September 5, 1866)

Article X and XI of impeachment against Johnson refer-
ence his "intemperate harangues" against Congress and
other verbal abuses. In this excerpt from a cross-country
speaking tour dubbed the Swing Around the Circle,
Johnson demonstrates such a harangue, lambasting po-
litical opponents and abandoning all pretense of presi-
dential decorum. Johnson even goes so far as to suggest
that a Republican senator should be hanged. Critics mostly
panned his speeches, and Johnson's party suffered in the
midterm elections.

On the arrival of the President at Cleveland, Ohio, on Mon-
day night, the party proceeded to the Kennard House, where
they sat down to supper. The crowd in front of the hotel becoming impatient and clamorous, and not being appeased by
the attempt to soothe them with music, the President appeared
and addressed them as follows:—

> *Fellow-citizens* . . .
> I am free to say that I am flattered by the demon-
> strations I have witnessed, and being flattered I don't

mean to think it personal, but as an evidence of what is pervading the public mind, and this demonstration is nothing more nor less than an indication of the latent sentiment or feeling of the great masses of the people. With regard to the proper settlement of this great question, I come before you as an American citizen simply, and not as the chief magistrate, clothed with the insignia and paraphernalia of state, being an inhabitant of a state of this union. . . .

. . . I want to say this, that I have lived among the American people and have represented them in some public capacity for the last twenty-five years, and where is the man or woman who can place his finger upon any single act of mine deviating from any pledge of mine, or in violation of the Constitution of the country? [Cheers.] Who is he? What language does he speak? What religion does he profess? Who can come and place his finger upon one pledge I ever violated or one principle I ever proved false to? [A voice—"How about New Orleans?" Another voice—"Hang Jeff Davis."] . . .

In presenting the few remarks that I designed to make, my intention was to address myself to your common sense, your judgment and your better feelings, not to the passion and malignity of your hearts. [Cheers.]

This was my object in presenting myself on this occasion, and to ask you how you do, and at the same time to bid you good night. In this assembly here tonight the remark has been made, "Traitor!" "Traitor!" My countrymen, will you hear me? [Shouts of yes.] And will you hear me for my cause and for the Constitution of my country? [Applause.] I want to know when or where, or under what circumstances Andrew Johnson . . . in any capacity, ever deserted any principle or violated the Constitution of his country. [Cries of "Never."]

Let me ask this large and intelligent audience if your Secretary of State, who served four years under Mr. Lincoln, and who was placed upon the butcher's block, as it were, and hacked to pieces and scarred by the assassin's knife, ever turned traitor? . . . If I were disposed to play the orator, and deal in declamation to-night, I would imitate one of the ancient tragedies, and would take William H. Seward and bring him before you, and point you to the hacks and scars upon his person. [A voice—"God bless him."] I would exhibit the bloody garments, saturated with gore from his gushing wounds; then I would ask you, why not hang Thad Stevens and Wendell Phillips?

I tell you, my country men, I have been fighting the South, and they have been whipped and crushed, and they acknowledge their defeat and accept the terms of the Constitution and now as I go around the circle having fought traitors at the South, I am prepared to fight traitors at the North. . . . God willing, with your help, we will do it. It will be crushed, North and South and this glorious union of ours will be preserved. [Cheers.] . . .

I do not come here as the chief magistrate of twenty-five States, but of thirty-six. [Cheers.] I come here to-night with the flag of my country and the Constitution of thirty-six States untarnished. Are you for dividing this country? [Cries of "No."]

Then I am President, and I am President of the United States. [Cheers.] I will tell you one other thing. I understand the discordant notes in this crowd to-night. He who is opposed to the restoration of this government and the reunion of the States is as great a traitor as Jeff Davis or Wendell Phillips. [Cheers.] I am against both. Some of you talk about traitors in the South who have no courage to get away from your home and fight them. [Laughter and cheers.]

The courageous men, Grant, Sherman, Farragut, and the long list of the distinguished sons of the Union were in the field, and led . . . to conquest and to victory, while you remained cowardly at home. [Applause.] Now when these brave men have returned home, many of whom have left an arm, or a leg, or their blood upon many a battlefield, they find you at home speculating and committing frauds on the government. [Laughter and cheers.]

You pretend now to have great respect and sympathy for the poor, brave fellow who has left an arm on the battlefield. [Cries—"Is this dignified?"] I understand you; you may talk about the dignity of the President. . . . I have been with you in the battles of this country, and I can tell you, furthermore, tonight, who has to pay these brave men who shed their blood. . . .

But, fellow citizens, let this all pass. I care not for my dignity. . . . A certain portion of our countrymen will respect a citizen whenever he is entitled to respect. . . . There is another of them that have no respect for themselves, and consequently they cannot respect anyone else. [Laughter and cheers.] . . .

When encroached upon, I care not from what quarter it comes, it is entitled to resistance. As chief magistrate I felt so after taking the oath to support the Constitution and when I saw encroachments upon your Constitution and rights, as an honest man, I dared to sound the tocsin of alarm. [Three cheers for Andrew Johnson.] . . . Let me say to those who thirst for more blood, who are still willing to sacrifice human life, if you want a victim and my country requires it, erect your altar and lay me upon it, to give the last libation to human freedom. [Loud applause.] . . .

In conclusion, Beside that Congress had taken great pains to poison their constituents against him. what had Congress done?—have they done anything to restore the union of these States? No; on the contrary, they had done everything to prevent it; and because he stood now where he had been when the rebellion commenced he had been denounced as a traitor.

Who had run greater risks or made grater sacrifices than himself? But Congress, factious and domineering, had undertaken to poison the minds of the American people. . . .

This gang of office holders, these bloodsuckers and cormorants, had got fat on the country. You have got them over your district, hence you see a system of legislation proposed so that these men shall not be turned out, and the President, the only channel through which they can be reached is called a tyrant. . . .

. . . All [I] wanted when war was over, and peace had come, for patriotic and Christian men to rally round the flag of the country in a fraternal hug, and resolve that all shall perish rather than that the Union shall not be restored.

"A Treacherous President Stood in the Way," by Frederick Douglass (1866)

> *Frederick Douglass was one of the most famous civil rights leaders and orators of his day. A formerly enslaved person, Douglass brought personal experience and moral clarity to the debate over slavery. He was not formally involved in the impeachment of Andrew Johnson. But in this critique of Johnson, written in* The Atlantic, *he encapsulates the moral failings of Johnson's presidency— far better than impeachment articles narrowly focused on the Tenure of Office Act. Douglass does not specifically call for impeachment here. However, his explanation of how the "treacherous" President Johnson failed the Constitution by opposing equal rights and advancing white supremacy would have provided strong grounds for impeachment.*

Seldom has any legislative body been the subject of a solicitude more intense, or of aspirations more sincere and ardent. There are the best of reasons for this profound interest. Questions of vast moment, left undecided by the last session of Congress, must be manfully grappled with by this. No political skirmishing will avail. The occasion demands statesmanship.

. . . The Civil Rights Bill and the Freedmen's Bureau Bill and the proposed constitutional amendments, with the amendment already adopted and recognized as the law of the land, do not reach the difficulty, and cannot, unless the whole structure of the government is changed from a government by States to something like a despotic central government, with power to control even the municipal regulations of States, and to make them conform to its own despotic will. While there remains such an idea as the right of each State to control its own local affairs,—an idea, by the way, more deeply rooted in the minds of men of all sections of the country than perhaps any one other political idea,—no general assertion of human rights can be of any practical value. To change the character of the government at this point is neither possible nor desirable. All that is necessary to be done is to make the government consistent with itself, and render the rights of the States compatible with the sacred rights of human nature.

The arm of the Federal government is long, but it is far too short to protect the rights of individuals in the interior of distant States. They must have the power to protect themselves, or they will go unprotected, spite of all the laws the Federal Government can put upon the national statute-book.

. . . The true way and the easiest way is to make our government entirely consistent with itself, and give to every loyal citizen the elective franchise,—a right and power which will be ever present, and will form a wall of fire for his protection.

One of the invaluable compensations of the late Rebellion is the highly instructive disclosure it made of the true source of danger to republican government. Whatever may be tolerated in monarchical and despotic governments, no republic is safe that tolerates a privileged class, or denies to any of its citizens equal rights and equal means to maintain them. What was theory before the war has been made fact by the war. . . .

It is asked, said Henry Clay, on a memorable occasion, will

slavery never come to an end? That question, said he, was asked fifty years ago, and it has been answered by fifty years of unprecedented prosperity. Spite of the eloquence of the earnest Abolitionists,—poured out against slavery during thirty years,— even they must confess, that, in all the probabilities of the case, that system of barbarism would have continued its horrors far beyond the limits of the nineteenth century but for the Rebellion, and perhaps only have disappeared at last in a fiery conflict, even more fierce and bloody than that which has now been suppressed.

... At any rate, to this grand work of national regeneration and entire purification Congress must now address itself, with full purpose that the work shall this time be thoroughly done. The deadly upas, root and branch, leaf and fibre, body and sap, must be utterly destroyed. The country is evidently not in a condition to listen patiently to pleas for postponement, however plausible, nor will it permit the responsibility to be shifted to other shoulders. Authority and power are here commensurate with the duty imposed. ...

If time was at first needed, Congress has now had time. All the requisite materials from which to form an intelligent judgment are now before it. Whether its members look at the origin, the progress, the termination of the war, or at the mockery of a peace now existing, they will find only one unbroken chain of argument in favor of a radical policy of reconstruction. For the omissions of the last session, some excuses may be allowed. A treacherous President stood in the way; and it can be easily seen how reluctant good men might be to admit an apostasy which involved so much of baseness and ingratitude. It was natural that they should seek to save him by bending to him even when he leaned to the side of error. But all is changed now. Congress knows now that it must go on without his aid, and even against his machinations. The advantage of the present session over the last is immense. ... The members go to

Washington fresh from the inspiring presence of the people. In every considerable public meeting, and in almost every conceivable way, whether at court-house, school-house, or crossroads, in doors and out, the subject has been discussed, and the people have emphatically pronounced in favor of a radical policy. Listening to the doctrines of expediency and compromise with pity, impatience, and disgust, they have everywhere broken into demonstrations of the wildest enthusiasm when a brave word has been spoken in favor of equal rights and impartial suffrage. Radicalism, so far from being odious, is now the popular passport to power. The men most bitterly charged with it go to Congress with the largest majorities, while the timid and doubtful are sent by lean majorities, or else left at home. The strange controversy between the President and Congress, at one time so threatening, is disposed of by the people. The high reconstructive powers which he so confidently, ostentatiously, and haughtily claimed, have been disallowed, denounced, and utterly repudiated; while those claimed by Congress have been confirmed.

Of the spirit and magnitude of the canvass nothing need be said. The appeal was to the people, and the verdict was worthy of the tribunal. Upon an occasion of his own selection, with the advice and approval of his astute Secretary, soon after the members of Congress had returned to their constituents, the President quitted the executive mansion, sandwiched himself between two recognized heroes,—men whom the whole country delighted to honor,—and, with all the advantage which such company could give him, stumped the country from the Atlantic to the Mississippi, advocating everywhere his policy as against that of Congress. It was a strange sight, and perhaps the most disgraceful exhibition ever made by any President; but, as no evil is entirely unmixed, good has come of this, as from many others. Ambitious, unscrupulous, energetic, indefatigable, voluble, and plausible,—a political gladiator,

ready for a "set-to" in any crowd,—he is beaten in his own chosen field, and stands to-day before the country as a convicted
usurper, a political criminal, guilty of a bold and persistent
attempt to possess himself of the legislative powers solemnly
secured to Congress by the Constitution. No vindication
could be more complete, no condemnation could be more absolute and humiliating. Unless reopened by the sword, as reck-
lessly threatened in some circles, this question is now closed
for all time.

    . . . [It] is obvious to common sense that the rebellious
States stand to-day, in point of law, precisely where they stood
when, exhausted, beaten, conquered, they fell powerless at the
feet of Federal authority. Their State governments were overthrown, and the lives and property of the leaders of the Rebellion were forfeited. In reconstructing the institutions of these
shattered and overthrown States, Congress should begin with
a clean slate, and make clean work of it. Let there be no hesi-
tation. It would be a cowardly deference to a defeated and
treacherous President, if any account were made of the illegit-
imate, one-sided, sham governments hurried into existence for
a malign purpose in the absence of Congress. These pretended
governments, which were never submitted to the people, and
from participation in which four millions of the loyal people
were excluded by Presidential order, should now be treated according to their true character, as shams and impositions, and
supplanted by true and legitimate governments, in the formation of which loyal men, black and white, shall participate.

    It is not, however, within the scope of this paper to point
out the precise steps to be taken, and the means to be employed.
The people are less concerned about these than the grand end
to be attained. They demand such a reconstruction as shall put
an end to the present anarchical state of things in the late rebellious States,—where frightful murders and wholesale mas-
sacres are perpetrated in the very presence of Federal soldiers.

This horrible business they require shall cease. . . . The South must be opened to the light of law and liberty, and this session of Congress is relied upon to accomplish this important work.

The plain, common-sense way of doing this work, as intimated at the beginning, is simply to establish in the South one law, one government, one administration of justice, one condition to the exercise of the elective franchise, for men of all races and colors alike. This great measure is sought as earnestly by loyal white men as by loyal blacks, and is needed alike by both. Let sound political prescience but take the place of an unreasoning prejudice, and this will be done.

Men denounce the negro for his prominence in this discussion; but it is no fault of his that in peace as in war, that in conquering Rebel armies as in reconstructing the rebellious States, the right of the negro is the true solution of our national troubles. The stern logic of events, which goes directly to the point, disdaining all concern for the color or features of men, has determined the interests of the country as identical with and inseparable from those of the negro.

The policy that emancipated and armed the negro—now seen to have been wise and proper by the dullest—was not certainly more sternly demanded than is now the policy of enfranchisement. If with the negro was success in war, and without him failure, so in peace it will be found that the nation must fall or flourish with the negro.

Fortunately, the Constitution of the United States knows no distinction between citizens on account of color. Neither does it know any difference between a citizen of a State and a citizen of the United States. Citizenship evidently includes all the rights of citizens, whether State or national. If the Constitution knows none, it is clearly no part of the duty of a Republican Congress now to institute one. The mistake of the last session was the attempt to do this very thing, by a renunciation of its power to secure political rights to any class of citizens, with the obvious purpose to allow the rebellious States to disfranchise, if they should see fit, their colored citizens. This unfortunate blunder must now be retrieved, and the emasculated citizenship given to the negro supplanted by that contemplated in the Constitution of the United States, which declares that the citizens of each State shall enjoy all the rights and immunities of citizens of the several States,—so that a legal voter in any State shall be a legal voter in all the States.

"Third Annual Message to Congress," by Andrew Johnson (December 3, 1867)

By December of 1867, Johnson was a weakened president, his Democratic Party having suffered serious defeats in the 1866 midterm elections. Instead of joining Republicans in fighting for the rights of newly freed blacks, Johnson doubled down on this opposition. In this message, he continues defending white supremacy, claiming the freedmen are not educated enough to vote and that civil rights legislation would create "negro domination." Johnson repeatedly references what he sees as his obligations to the Constitution and the Union in his defenses of states' rights. But for some in Congress, the speech was further proof that Johnson was the one violating his constitutional oath.

Fellow-Citizens of the Senate and House of Representatives: . . .

When a civil war has been brought to a close, it is manifestly the first interest and duty of the state to repair the injuries which the war has inflicted, and to secure the benefit of the lessons it teaches as fully and as speedily as possible. This duty was, upon the termination of the rebellion, promptly accepted not only by the executive department, but by the insurrectionary States themselves, and restoration in the first moment of peace was believed to be as easy and certain as it was indispensable. The expectations, however, then so reasonably and confidently entertained were disappointed by legislation from which I felt constrained by my obligations to the Constitution to withhold my assent.

It is therefore a source of profound regret that in complying with the obligation imposed upon the President by the Constitution to give to Congress from time to time information of the state of the Union I am unable to communicate any definitive adjustment satisfactory to the American people, of the questions which since the close of the rebellion have agitated the public mind. On the contrary, candor compels me to declare that at this time there is no Union as our fathers understood the term, and as they meant it to be understood by us.

The Union which they established can exist only where all the States are represented in both Houses of Congress; where one State is as free as another to regulate its internal concerns according to its own will, and where the laws of the central Government, strictly confined to matters of national jurisdiction, apply with equal force to all the people of every section. That such is not the present "state of the Union" is a melancholy fact . . .

The Union and the Constitution are inseparable. As long as one is obeyed by all parties, the other will be preserved; and if one is destroyed, both must perish together. The destruction of the Constitution will be followed by other and still greater calamities. . . . Nothing but implicit obedience to its requirements in all parts of the country will accomplish these great ends. Without that obedience we can look forward only to continual outrages upon individual rights, incessant breaches of the public peace, national weakness, financial dishonor, the total loss of our prosperity, the general corruption of morals, and the final extinction of popular freedom. . . .

To me the process of restoration seems perfectly plain and

simple. It consists merely in a faithful application of the Constitution and laws. . . . All the rights and all the obligations of States and individuals can be protected and enforced by means perfectly consistent with the fundamental law. . . .

It is clear to my apprehension that the States lately in rebellion are still members of the National Union. When did they cease to be so? The "ordinances of secession" adopted by a portion (in most of them a very small portion) of their citizens were mere nullities. . . . It can not be that a successful war, waged for the preservation of the Union, had the legal effect of dissolving it. . . . To dissolve the Union is to repeal the Constitution which holds it together, and that is a power which does not belong to any department of this Government, or to all of them united. . . .

If the Southern States are component parts of the Union, the Constitution is the supreme law for them, as it is for all the other States. They are bound to obey it, and so are we. . . . Without the Constitution we are nothing; by, through, and under the Constitution we are what it makes us. . . .

Being sincerely convinced that these views are correct, I would be unfaithful to my duty if I did not recommend the repeal of the acts of Congress which place ten of the Southern States under the domination of military masters. . . .

I am aware it is assumed that this system of government for the Southern States is not to be perpetual. It is true this military government is to be only provisional, but it is through this temporary evil that a greater evil is to be made perpetual. If the guaranties of the Constitution can be broken provisionally to serve a temporary purpose, and in a part only of the country, we can destroy them everywhere and for all time. . . . The States that are still free may be enslaved at any moment; for if the Constitution does not protect all, it protects none.

It is manifestly and avowedly the object of these laws to confer upon Negroes the privilege of voting and to disfranchise such a number of white citizens as will give the former a clear majority at all elections in the Southern States. This, to the minds of some persons, is so important that a violation of the Constitution is justified as a means of bringing it about. The morality is always false which excuses a wrong because it proposes to accomplish a desirable end. We are not permitted to do evil that good may come. But in this case the end itself is evil, as well as the means.

The subjugation of the States to Negro domination would be worse than the military despotism under which they are now suffering. It was believed beforehand that the people would endure any amount of military oppression for any length of time rather than degrade themselves by subjection to the Negro race. . . . Negro suffrage was established by act of Congress, and the military officers were commanded to superintend the process of clothing the Negro race with the political privileges torn from white men.

The blacks in the South are entitled to be well and humanely governed, and to have the protection of just laws for all their rights of person and property. If it were practicable at this time to give them a Government exclusively their own, under which they might manage their own affairs in their own way, it would become a grave question whether we ought to do so, or whether common humanity would not require us to save them from themselves. But under the circumstances this is only a speculative point. It is not proposed merely that they shall govern themselves, but that they shall rule the white race, make and administer State laws, elect Presidents and members of Congress, and shape to a greater or less extent the future destiny of the whole country. Would such a trust and power be safe in such hands? . . .

In the Southern States, however, Congress has undertaken to confer upon them the privilege of the ballot. Just released from slavery, it may be doubted whether as a class they know more than their ancestors how to organize and regulate civil society. Indeed, it is admitted that the blacks of the South are not only regardless of the rights of property, but so utterly ignorant of public affairs that their voting can consist in nothing more than carrying a ballot to the place where they are directed to deposit it. . . .

. . . Yesterday, as it were, 4,000,000 persons were held in a condition of slavery that had existed for generations; to-day they are freemen and are assumed by law to be citizens. It can not be presumed, from their previous condition of servitude, that as a class they are as well informed as to the nature of our Government as the intelligent foreigner who makes our land the home of his choice. . . . In the hands of the patriotic and worthy our Government will be preserved upon the principles of the Constitution inherited from our fathers. It follows, therefore, that in admitting to the ballot box a new class of voters not qualified for the exercise of the elective franchise we weaken our system of government instead of adding to its strength and durability. . . .

I repeat the expression of my willingness to join in any plan within the scope of our constitutional authority which promises to better the condition of the Negroes in the South, by encouraging them in industry, enlightening their minds, improving their morals, and giving protection to all their just rights as freedmen. But the transfer of our political inheritance to them would, in my opinion, be an abandonment of a duty which we owe alike to the memory of our fathers and the rights of our children. . . .

. . . We must not delude ourselves. . . . It is vain to hope that Negroes will maintain their ascendency themselves. Without military power they are wholly incapable of holding in subjection the white people of the South. . . .

The great interests of the country require immediate relief from these enactments. Business in the South is paralyzed by a sense of general insecurity, by the terror of confiscation, and the dread of Negro supremacy. The Southern trade, from which the North would have derived so great a profit under a government of law, still languishes, and can never be revived until it ceases to be fettered by the arbitrary power which makes all its operations unsafe. . . . We live in a country where the popular will always enforces obedience to itself, sooner or later. . . . It can not have escaped your attention that from the day on which Congress fairly and formally presented the proposition to govern the Southern States by military force, with a view to the ultimate establishment of Negro supremacy, every expression of the general sentiment has been more or less adverse to it. . . . Their determination to preserve the inheritance of free government in their own hands and transmit it undivided and unimpaired to their own posterity is too strong to be successfully opposed. Every weaker passion will disappear before that love of liberty and law for which the American people are distinguished above all others in the world.

How far the duty of the President "to preserve, protect, and defend the Constitution" requires him to go in opposing an unconstitutional act of Congress is a very serious and important question, on which I have deliberated much and felt extremely anxious to reach a proper conclusion. . . . Cases may occur in which the Executive would be compelled to stand on its rights, and maintain them regardless of all consequences. If Congress should pass an act which is not only in palpable conflict with the Constitution, but will certainly, if carried out, produce immediate and irreparable injury to the organic structure of the Government, and if there be neither judicial remedy for the wrongs it inflicts nor power in the people to protect themselves without the official aid of their elected defender . . . in such a case the President must take the high responsibilities of his office and save the life of the nation at all hazards. . . .

It is well and publicly known that enormous frauds have

been perpetrated on the Treasury and that colossal fortunes have been made at the public expense. This species of corruption has increased, is increasing, and if not diminished will soon bring us into total ruin and disgrace. . . . The system, never perfected, was much disorganized by the "tenure-of-office bill," which has almost destroyed official accountability. The President may be thoroughly convinced that an officer is incapable, dishonest, or unfaithful to the Constitution, but under the law which I have named the utmost he can do is to complain to the Senate and ask the privilege of supplying his place with a better man. . . . I am entirely persuaded that under such a rule the President can not perform the great duty assigned to him of seeing the laws faithfully executed, and that it disables him most especially from enforcing that rigid accountability which is necessary to the due execution of the revenue laws.

Articles of Impeachment Against Andrew Johnson (February 24, 1868)

The House of Representatives, jumping quickly into action after Johnson fired Secretary of War Edwin Stanton, voted 126 to 47 to impeach President Johnson. This vote marked the first time in U.S. history a president had been impeached. Ultimately, eleven articles of impeachment were approved. The first nine dealt with different aspects of the Stanton firing, with significant overlap. Yet some representatives were unsatisfied, thinking Johnson's offenses transcended this one legal violation. They worked in a tenth article focusing on the president's vitriolic speeches, and an omnibus eleventh article that summarized a multitude of Congress's complaints with Johnson. An abridged selection of the key articles is below.

ARTICLE 1. That said Andrew Johnson, President of the United States, . . . unmindful of the high duties of his oath of office and of the requirements of the Constitution that he should take care that the laws be faithfully executed, did unlawfully, . . . issue an order in writing for the removal of Edwin M. Stanton from the office of Secretary of the Department of War . . .

Which order was unlawfully issued, and with intent then are there to violate the act entitled "An act regulating the tenure of certain civil office," passed March 2, 1867, and contrary to the provisions of said act, and in violation thereof, and contrary to the provisions of the Constitution of the United States, and without the advice and consent of the Senate of the United States, the said Senate then and there being in session, to remove said E. M. Stanton from the office of Secretary for the Department of War, whereby said Andrew Johnson, President of the United States, did then and there commit, and was guilty of a high misdemeanor in office. . . .

ARTICLE 3. . . . That without authority of law, while the Senate of the United States was then and there in session, he did appoint one Lorenzo Thomas to be Secretary for the Department of War, ad interim, without the advice and consent of the Senate . . .

ARTICLE 4. That said Andrew Johnson, President of the United States, . . . did unlawfully conspire with one Lorenzo Thomas, and with other persons to the House of Representatives unknown, with intent, by intimidation and threats, to hinder and prevent Edwin M. Stanton, then and there, the Secretary for the Department of War, duly appointed under the laws of the United States, from holding said office of Secretary for the Department of War . . .

ARTICLE 6. That Andrew Johnson, President of the United States, . . . did unlawfully conspire with one Lorenzo Thomas, by force to seize, take and possess the property of the United Sates at the War Department, contrary to the provisions of an act entitled "An act to define and punish certain conspiracies," approved July 31, 1861, and with intent to violate and disregard an act entitled "An act regulating the tenure of certain civil offices," passed March 2, 1867 . . .

ARTICLE 7. That said Andrew Johnson, President of the United States, . . . did unlawfully conspire with one Lorenzo Thomas to prevent and hinder the execution of an act of the United States, entitled "An act regulating the tenure of certain civil office," passed March 2, 1867, and in pursuance of said conspiracy, did unlawfully attempt to prevent Edwin M. Stanton, then and there being Secretary for the Department of War, under the laws of the United States, from holding said office to which he had been duly appointed and commissioned . . .

ARTICLE 10. That said Andrew Johnson . . . unmindful of the . . . harmony and courtesies which ought to exist and be maintained between the executive and legislative branches of the Government of the United States, designing and intending to set aside the rightful authorities and powers of Congress, did attempt to bring into disgrace, ridicule, hatred, contempt and reproach, the Congress of the United States, and the several branches thereof, to impair and destroy the regard and respect of all the good people of the United States for the Congress and the legislative power thereof . . .

Which said utterances, declarations, threats and harangues, highly censurable in any, are peculiarly indecent and unbecoming in the Chief Magistrate of the United States, by means whereof the said Andrew Johnson has brought the high office of the President of the United States into contempt, ridicule and disgrace, to the great scandal of all good citizens . . .

ARTICLE 11. That the said Andrew Johnson . . . did, heretofore, to wit: On the 18th day of August, 1866, at the city of Washington, and in the District of Columbia, by public speech, declare and affirm in substance, that the Thirty-ninth Congress of the United States was not a Congress of the United States authorized by the Constitution to exercise legislative power under the same, but on the contrary, was a Congress of only part of the States, thereby denying and intending to deny, that the legislation of said Congress was valid or obligatory upon him, the said Andrew Johnson, except in so far as he saw fit to approve the same, and also thereby denying the power of the said Thirty-ninth Congress to propose amendments to the Constitution of the United States.

Closing Argument of the House Managers for Impeachment, delivered by John Bingham (May 6, 1868)

The Constitution does not offer a specific guide for how an impeachment trial is supposed to operate in the Senate. In the Johnson impeachment trial, senators, with Chief Justice Salmon P. Chase presiding, decided that a small group on each side would press the case for Johnson or for his impeachment. Representative John Bingham of Ohio was chosen as one of the "managers" for the impeachment side. Johnson's personal lawyers would come to his defense. In this closing argument, the formerly moderate Bingham delivers a ringing indictment of Johnson for failing to live up to his oath of office, venturing far beyond the Tenure of Office case to show how Johnson violated the public trust.

. . . These are the offences with which [the President] stands charged. They have acquired and taken something of technical form and shape in the articles; but the effect of the charges against the President is usurpation in office, suspending the people's laws, dispensing with the execution thereof purposely, with intent to violate them, and, in the language of the article, to hinder and to prevent their execution.

The attempted avoidance set up is an implied judicial power, as it was called by the learned counsel of the President, to determine for himself the true construction of the Constitution, and judicially to determine for himself the validity of all your laws. I have endeavored to show, senators, that this assumption of the President is incompatible with every provision of your Constitution; that it is at war with all the traditions of the republic; that it is in direct conflict with the contemporaneous and continued construction of the Constitution by the legislative, executive, and judicial departments. I have endeavored also to impress you, senators, with my own conviction that this assumption of the President to interpret the Constitution and the laws for himself, to suspend the execution of the laws at his pleasure, is an assumption of power simply to set aside the Constitution, to set aside the laws, and to annihilate the government of the people. This is the President's crime: that he has assumed this prerogative, dangerous to the people's liberties, violative alike of his oath, of the Constitution, and of the laws enacted under the Constitution. . . .

And yet the President has the audacity in his answer—and I go not beyond it to convict him—to come before the Senate and declare in substance: "Admitting all that is charged against me to be true . . . nevertheless, I say it was my right to do so, and it is not your right to hold me to answer, because by force of the Constitution I am entitled to interpret the Constitution for myself, and to decide upon the validity of a law, whether it conflicts with a power conferred upon me by the Constitution, and if it does, I must take the necessary steps to test its validity in the courts of justice." . . .

. . . I do not propose to repeat my argument, but I ask the Senate to consider, that if the courts shall be allowed to intervene, and in the first instance decide any question of this sort between the people and the accused President, it necessarily does result that the courts at last, acting upon the suggestions of the President, may decide every question of impeachment which can possibly arise by reason of the malfeasance and guilty acts of a President in office, and defy the power of the people to impeach him and try him in the Senate. . . .

These acts charged, then, as I said, are acts of usurpation in office, criminal violations of the Constitution and laws of the land; and inasmuch as they are committed by the Chief Magistrate of the nation, dangerous to the public liberties. The people, have declared in words too plain to be mistaken, and too strong to be evaded by the subtleties of a false logic, that the Constitution ordained by them, and the laws enacted by their representatives in Congress assembled, shall be obeyed, and shall be executed and enforced by their servant, the President of the United States, until the same shall be amended or repealed in the mode prescribed by themselves. They have written this decree of theirs all over this land in the tempest and fire of battle.

When twelve million people, standing within the limits of eleven States of this Union, entered into confederation and agreement against the supremacy of the Constitution and laws, and conspired to suspend their execution and to annul them within their respective territorial limits, from ocean to ocean, by a sublime uprising, the people stamped out in blood the atrocious assumption that millions of men were to be permitted, acting under State organizations, to suspend for a moment the supremacy of the Constitution or the execution of the people's laws. Is it to be supposed that this great and triumphant people, who but yesterday wrote this decree of theirs amid the flame of battle, are now at this day tamely to submit to the same assumption of power by a single man, and he their own sworn Executive? Let the people, answer that question, as they assuredly will answer it, in the coming elections.

Is it not in vain, I ask you that the people have thus vindicated by battle the supremacy of their own Constitution and laws, if, after all, their President is permitted to suspend their laws and dispense with the execution thereof at pleasure, and defy the power of the people to bring him to trial and punishment before the only tribunal authorized by the Constitution to try him? That is the issue which is presented before the Senate for decision by these articles of impeachment. By such acts of usurpation on the part of the ruler of a people, I need not say to the Senate, the peace of nations is broken, as it is only by obedience to law that the peace of nations is maintained and their existence perpetuated. . . .

Senators, it is the pride and boast of that great people from whom we are descended, as it is the pride and boast of every American, that the law is the supreme power of the state and is for the protection of each by the combined power of all. By the constitution of England the hereditary monarch is no more above the law than the humblest subject; and by the Constitution of the United States the President is no more above the law than the poorest and most friendless beggar in your streets. . . .

. . . May God forbid that the future historian shall record of this day's proceedings, that by reason of the failure of the legislative power of the people to triumph over the usurpations of an apostate President through the defection of the Senate of the United States, the just and great fabric of American empire fell and perished from the earth! . . .

. . . Without revolution, senators, like the great Parliament of 1688, you are asked to reassert the principles of the Constitution of your country, not to be searched for through the statutes of centuries, but to be found in that grand, sacred, written instrument given to us by the fathers of the republic. . . . It was ordained by the people of the United States amid the convulsions and agonies of nations. By its express provisions all men within its jurisdiction are equal before the law, equally entitled to those rights of person which are as universal as the material structure of one man, and equally liable to answer to its tribunals of justice for every injury done either to the citizen or to the state.

It is this spirit of justice, of liberty, of equality, that makes your Constitution dear to freemen in this and in all lands, in that it secures to every man his rights, and to the people at large the inestimable right of self-government, the right which is this day challenged by this usurping President, for if he be a law to himself the people are no longer their own law-makers through their representatives in Congress assembled; the President thereby simply becomes their dictator. If the President becomes a dictator he will become so by the judgment of the Senate, not by the text of the Constitution, not by any interpretation heretofore put upon it by any act of the people, nor by any act of the people's representatives. The representatives of the people have discharged their duty in his impeachment. They have presented him at the bar of the Senate for trial, in that he has usurped and attempted to combine in himself the legislative and judicial powers of this great people, thereby claiming for himself a power by which he may annihilate their government. We have seen that when the supremacy of their Constitution was challenged by battle, the people made such sacrifice to maintain it as has no parallel in history.

Can it be that after this triumph of law over anarchy, of right over wrong, of patriotism over treason, the Constitution and laws are again to be assailed in the capital of the nation in the person of the Chief Magistrate, and by the judgment of the Senate he is to be protected in that usurpation? The President by his answer and by the representations of his counsel asks you, deliberately asks you, by your judgment to set the accused above the Constitution which he has violated and above the people whom he has betrayed . . .

I ask you, senators, how long men would deliberate upon the question whether criminal violation of the law, should be permitted to interpose a plea in justification of his criminal act that his only purpose was to interpret the Constitution and laws for himself, that he violated the law in the exercise of his prerogative to test its validity hereafter at such day as might suit his own convenience in the courts of justice. Surely, senators, it is as competent for the private citizen to interpose such justification in answer to crime in one of your tribunals of justice as it is for the President of the United States to interpose it, and for the simple reason that the Constitution is no respecter of persons and vests neither in the President nor in the private citizen judicial power.

Pardon me for saying it; I speak it in no offensive spirit; I speak it from a sense of duty; I utter but my own conviction, and desire to place it upon the record, that for the Senate to sustain any such plea, would, in my judgment, be a gross violation of the already violated Constitution and laws of a free people. . . .

I put away the possibility that the Senate of the United States, equal in dignity to any tribunal in the world, is capable of recording any such decision even upon the petition and prayer of this accused and guilty President. Can it be that by reason of his great office the President is to be protected in his high crimes and misdemeanors, violative alike of his oath, of the Constitution, and of the express letter of your written law enacted by the legislative department of the government? . . .

. . . I ask you to consider that I speak before you this day in behalf of the violated law of a free people who commission me. I ask you to remember that I speak this day under the obligations of my oath. I ask you to consider that I am not insensible to the significance of the words of which mention was made by the learned counsel from New York: justice, duty, law, oath. I ask you to remember that the great principles of constitutional liberty for which I this day speak have been taught to men and nations by all the trials and triumphs, by all the agonies and martyrdoms of the past; that they are the wisdom of the centuries uttered by the elect of the human race who were made perfect through suffering.

I ask you to consider that we stand this day pleading for the violated majesty of the law, by the graves of a half million of martyred hero-patriots who made death beautiful by the sacrifice of themselves for their country, the Constitution, and the laws, and who, by their sublime example, have taught us that all must obey the law; that none are above the law; that no man lives for himself alone, but each for all; that some must die that the state may live; that the citizen is at best but for to-day, while the Commonwealth is for all time; and that position, however high, patronage, however powerful, cannot be permitted to shelter crime to the peril of the republic.

It only remains for me, senators, to thank you, as I do, for the honor you have done me by your kind attention, and to demand, in the name of the House of Representatives, and of the people of the United States, judgment against the accused for the high crimes and misdemeanors in office whereof he stands impeached, and of which before God and man he is guilty.

Opinion on the Impeachment Trial of Andrew Johnson, by Charles Sumner (May 16, 1868)

Charles Sumner of Massachusetts was an imposing fig-ure in the Senate—an icon among the Republicans for his steadfast commitment to the antislavery cause. He had earlier argued against a motion that senators should have to provide a written opinion on their impeachment vote. But having lost that battle, he fully embraced the task. This written opinion is a forthright critique of Johnson's most basic failings: that he fought on the side of slavery and violated the principles of separation of powers. Sumner also clearly lays out why impeachment must be seen as a punishment for political offenses, not legal ones.

BATTLE WITH SLAVERY

This is one of the last great battles with slavery. Driven from these legislative chambers, driven from the field of war, this monstrous power has found a refuge in the Executive Mansion, where, in utter disregard of the Constitution and laws, it seeks to exercise its ancient far-reaching sway. All this is very plain. Nobody can question it. Andrew Johnson is the impersonation of the tyrannical slave power. . . . Original partisans of slavery north and south; habitual compromisers of great principles; maligners of the Declaration of Independence; politicians without heart; lawyers, for whom a technicality is everything, and a promiscuous company who at every stage of the battle have set their faces against equal rights; these are his allies. . . . With the President at their head, they are now entrenched in Executive Mansion.

Not to dislodge them is to leave the country a prey to one of the most hateful tyrannies of history. Especially is it to surrender the Unionists of the rebel States to violence and bloodshed. Not a month, not a week, not a day should be lost. The safety of the Republic requires action at once. The lives of innocent men must be rescued from sacrifice.

I would not in this judgment depart from that moderation which belongs to the occasion; but God forbid that, when called to deal with so great an offender, I should affect a coldness which I cannot feel. Slavery has been our worst enemy, assailing all, murdering our children, filling our homes with mourning, and darkening the land with tragedy; and now it rears its crest anew, with Andrew Johnson as its representative. Through him it assumes once more to rule the Republic and to impose its cruel law. . . .

The formal accusation is founded on certain recent transgressions, enumerated in articles of impeachment, but it is wrong to suppose that this is the whole case. It is very wrong to try this impeachment merely on these articles. It is unpardonable to higgle over words and phrases when, for more than two years the tyrannical pretensions of this offender, now in evidence before the Senate, as I shall show, have been manifest in their terrible, heart-rending consequences. . . .

POLITICAL OFFENSES ARE
IMPEACHABLE OFFENSES

So much depends on the right understanding of the character of this proceeding, that even at the risk of protracting this discussion, I cannot hesitate to consider this branch of the subject, although what I have already said may render it superfluous. What are impeachable offences has been much considered in this trial, and sometimes with very little appreciation of the question. Next to the mystification from calling the Senate a court has been that other mystification from not calling the transgressions of Andrew Johnson impeachable offences. . . .

. . . If ever injuries were done immediately to society itself; if ever there was an abuse or violation of public trust; if ever there was misconduct of a public man; all these are now before us in the case of Andrew Johnson. The Federalist has been echoed ever since by all who have spoken with knowledge and without prejudice. . . .

OUTLINE OF TRANSGRESSIONS
OF ANDREW JOHNSON

. . . I pass now to the consideration of this overwhelming testimony and how the present impeachment became a necessity. I have already called it one of the last great battles with slavery. See now how the battle began.

Slavery in all its pretensions is a defiance of law; for it can have no law in its support. Whoso becomes its representative must act accordingly; and this is the transcendent crime of Andrew Johnson. For the sake of slavery and to uphold its original supporters in their endeavors to continue this wrong under another name, he has set at defiance the Constitution and laws of the land, and he has accompanied this unquestionable usurpation by brutalities and indecencies in office without precedent. . . . This usurpation with its brutalities and indecencies, became manifest as long ago as the winter of 1866, when, being President, and bound by his oath of office to preserve, protect, and defend the Constitution, and to take care that the laws are faithfully executed, he took to himself legislative powers in the reconstruction of the rebel

States, and, in carrying forward this usurpation, nullified an act of Congress, intended as the corner-stone of reconstruction, by virtue of which rebels are excluded from office under the government of the United States, and thereafter, in vindication of this misconduct, uttered a scandalous speech in which he openly charged members of Congress with being assassins, and mentioned some by name. Plainly he should have been impeached and expelled at that early day. The case against him was complete.

ACCUMULATION OF IMPEACHABLE OFFENSES

This is nothing but the outline, derived from historic sources which the Senate on this occasion is bound to recognize. Other acts fall within the picture. . . . The Freedman's Bureau, that sacred charity of the Republic, was despoiled of its possessions for the sake of rebels, to whom their forfeited estates were given back after they had been vested by law in the United States. . . . The pardoning power was prostituted, and pardons were issued in lots to suit rebels, thus grossly abusing that trust whose discreet exercise is so essential to the administration of justice. . . . The veto power conferred by the Constitution as a remedy for ill-considered legislation, was turned by him into a weapon of offence against Congress and into an instrument to beat down the just opposition which his usurpation had aroused. . . . Laws enacted by Congress for the benefit of the colored race, including that great statute for the establishment of the Freedmen's Bureau, and that other great statute for the establishment of Civil Rights, were first attacked by his veto, and, when finally passed by the requisite majority over his veto, were treated by him as little better than dead letters, while he boldly attempted to prevent the adoption of a constitutional amendment, by which the right of citizens and the national debt were placed under the guarantee of irrepealable law. . . .

OPEN DEFIANCE OF CONGRESS

For all these, or any one of them, Andrew Johnson should have been impeached and expelled from office. The case required a statement only; not an argument. Unhappily this was not done. . . . The field was narrow, but sufficient. There was but one thing for the House of Representatives to do. Andrew Johnson must be impeached, or the tenure-of-office act would become a dead letter, while his tyranny would receive a letter of license, and impeachment as a remedy for wrong-doing would be blotted from the Constitution. . . .

The articles themselves are narrow, if not technical. But they are filled and broadened by the transgressions of the past, all of which enter into the present offences. The whole is an unbroken series with a common life. . . .

ARTICLES OF IMPEACHMENT

In entering upon the discussion of the articles of impeachment, I confess my regret that so great a cause, on which so much depends, should be presented on such narrow ground, although I cannot doubt that the whole past must be taken into consideration in determining the character of the acts alleged. . . .

Of the transactions embraced by the articles, the removal of Mr. Stanton has unquestionably attracted the most attention, although I cannot doubt that the scandalous harangues are as justly worthy of condemnation. But the former has been made the pivot of this impeachment; so much so that the whole case seems to revolve on this transaction. Therefore I shall not err, if, following the articles, I put this foremost in the present inquiry. . . .

SWARM OF TECHNICALITIES AND QUIBBLES

I now come upon that swarm of technicalities, devices, quirks, and quibbles, which, from the beginning, have infested this great proceeding. . . . From these know all. In the face of presidential pretensions, inconsistent with constitutional liberty, the apologists have contributed their efforts to save the criminal by subtleties, which can secure his acquittal in form only, as by a flaw in an indictment, and they have done this, knowing that he will be left in power to assert his prerogative, and that his acquittal will be a new letter of license. . . . Every doubt, every scruple, every technicality, every subtlety, every quibble has been arrayed on his side, when, by every rule of reason and patriotism, all should have been arrayed on the side of our country. The Public Safety, which is the supreme law, is now imperiled. Are we not told by Blackstone that the law is always ready to catch at anything in favor of liberty? But these apologists catch at anything to save a usurper. . . .

Constantly we are admonished that we must confine ourselves to the articles. . . . Of course such a system of exclusion sacrifices justice, belittles this trial, and forgets that essential latitude I of inquiry which belongs to a political proceeding, having for its object expulsion from Office only and not punishment . . . This great offender should be seen in the light of day; precisely as he is; nor more, nor less; with nothing dwarfed; with no limits to the vision, and with all the immense background of accumulated transgressions filling the horizon as far as the eye can reach. The sight might ache; but how else can justice be done? . . .

GUILTY ON ALL THE ARTICLES

After this survey it is easy for me to declare how I shall vote. My duty will be to vote guilty on all the articles. If consistent with the rules of the Senate, I should vote, "Guilty of all and infinitely more." . . .

CONCLUSION

In the judgment which I now deliver I cannot hesitate. To my vision the path is clear as day. Never in history was there a great case more free from all just doubt. If Andrew Johnson is not guilty, then never was a political offender guilty before; and, if his acquittal is taken as a precedent, never can a political offender be found guilty again. The proofs are mountainous. Therefore, you are now determining whether impeachment shall continue a beneficent remedy in the Constitution, or be blotted out forever, and the country handed over to the terrible process of revolution as its sole protection. If the milder process cannot be made effective now, when will it ever be? . . .

The apologists are prone to remind the Senate that they are acting under the obligation of an oath. So are the rest of us, even if we do not ostentatiously declare it. By this oath, which is the same for all, we are sworn to do "impartial justice." It is justice, and this justice must be impartial. There must be no false weights and no exclusion of proper weights. Therefore, I cannot allow the jargon of lawyers on mere questions of form to sway this judgment against justice. Nor can I consent to shut out from view that long list of transgressions explaining and coloring the final act of defiance. To do so is not to render "impartial justice," but to depart from this golden rule. The oath we have taken is poorly kept if we forget the Public Safety in devices for the criminal. Above all else, now and forever, is that justice which "holds the scales of right with even hand." In this sacred name, and in the name also of country, that great charity embracing so many other charities, I now make this final protest against all questions of form at the expense of the Republic.

Something also has been said of the people, now watching our proceedings with patriotic solicitude, and it has been proclaimed that they are wrong to intrude their judgment. I do not think so. This is a political proceeding, which the people at this moment are as competent to decide as the Senate. They are the multitudinous jury, coming from no small vicinage, but from the whole country; for, on this impeachment, involving the Public Safety, the vicinage is the whole country. It is they who have sent us here, as their representatives, and in their name to consult for the common weal. In nothing can we escape their judgment, least of all on a question like that now before us. It is a mistake to suppose that the Senate only has heard the evidence. The people have heard it also, day by day, as it was delivered, and have carefully considered the case on its merits, properly dismissing all apologetic subtleties. It will be for them to review what has been done. They are above the Senate, and will "rejudge its justice." Thus it has been in other cases. The popular superstition, which long surrounded the

Supreme Court, could not save this tribunal from condemnation, amounting sometimes to execration, when, by an odious judgment, it undertook to uphold slavery; . . . The present trial, like that in the Supreme Court, is a battle with slavery. Acquittal is another Dred Scott decision, and another chapter in the Barbarism of Slavery. . . .

For myself, I cannot despair of the Republic. It is a lifeboat, which wind and wave cannot sink; but it may suffer much and be beaten by storms. All this I clearly see before us, if you fail to displace an unfit commander, whose power is a peril and a shame.

Part III

RICHARD NIXON

Transcript of a Conversation Between Richard Nixon, John Dean, and H. R. Haldeman (March 21, 1973)

Today we know that the Watergate burglars were paid hush money by people connected to President Nixon's re-election campaign. Our knowledge of the affair was made possible by a shocking fact: Richard Nixon had installed secret recording devices within the Oval Office of the White House. Nixon's tapes were released only after a drawn-out legal battle, culminating in the Supreme Court's ruling in United States v. Nixon *on July 24, 1974, which mandated that Nixon turn the tapes over to special prosecutor Leon Jaworski. The tapes proved disastrous for Nixon. After the famous "smoking gun" tape was released on August 5, days after the House Judiciary Committee approved two articles of impeachment, Nixon resigned. In this conversation, President Nixon discusses the Watergate scandal and hush payments with White House counsel John Dean and chief of staff H. R. Haldeman.*

[Discussing the purpose of the conversation]

Dean: The reason I thought we ought to talk this morning is because, in our conversations, I have the impression that you don't know everything I know, and it makes it very difficult for you to make judgments that only you can make—

Nixon: That's right. . . . in other words, I've got to know why you'd feel that our [*unclear*] something [*unclear*]—

Dean: Well, let me—

Nixon: —that we shouldn't unravel something.

Dean: Let me give you my overall, first.

Nixon: In other words, your judgment as to where it stands and where we ought to go.

Dean: I think that there's no doubt about the seriousness of the problem we've got. We have a cancer within—close to the presidency, that's growing. It's growing daily. It's compounding. It grows geometrically now, because it compounds itself.

That'll be clear as I explain, you know, some of the details of why it is, and it basically is because (1) we're being blackmailed, (2) people are going to start perjuring themselves very quickly that have not had to perjure themselves to protect other people, and the like. And that is just—and there is no assurance—

Nixon: That it won't bust.

Dean: That that won't bust.

Nixon: That's true.

———

[Discussing payouts and how to deal with the Watergate burglars]

Dean: Uh, Liddy said, said that, you know, if they [the burglars] all got counsel instantly and said that, you know', "We'll, ride this thing out." All right, then they started making demands. "We've got to have attorneys' fees. Uh, we don't have any money ourselves, and if—you are asking us to take this through the election." All right, so arrangements were made through Mitchell, uh, initiating it, in discussions that—I was present—that these guys had to be taken care of. Their attorneys' fees had to be done. Kalmbach was brought in. Uh, Kalmbach raised some cash. Uh, they were obv—, uh, you know—

Nixon: They put that under the cover of a Cuban Committee or [*unintelligible*].

Dean: Yeah, they, they had a Cuban Committee and they had—some of it was given to Hunt's lawyer, who in turn passed it out. This, you know, when Hunt's wife was flying to Chicago with ten thousand, she was actually, I understand after the fact now, was going to pass that money to, uh, one of the Cubans, to meet him in Chicago and pass it to somebody there.

Nixon: Why didn't she [*unintelligible*] maybe—well, whether it's maybe too late to do anything about it, but I would certainly keep that, [*laughs*] that cover for whatever it's worth. . . . Keep the Committee.

Dean: Af—, after, well, that, that . . . that's the most troublesome post-thing, uh, because (1) Bob is involved in that; John is involved in that; I'm involved in that; Mitchell is involved in that. And that's an obstruction of justice.

Nixon: In other words the fact that uh, that you're, you're, you're taking care of witnesses.

Dean: That's right ... Right. Uh, so that's, that's it. That's the, the extent of the knowledge. Now, where, where are the soft spots on this? Well, first of all, there's the, there's the problem of the continued blackmail

Nixon: Right.

Dean: ... which will not only go on now, it'll go on when these people are in prison, and it will compound the obstruction of justice situation. It'll cost money. It's dangerous. Nobody, nothing—people around here are not pros at this sort of thing. This is the sort of thing Mafia people can do: washing money, getting clean money, and things like that, uh—we're—we just don't know about those (noise) things, because we're not used to, you know—we are not criminals and not used to dealing in that business. ...

Nixon: That's right.

Dean: It's tough thing to know how to do.

Nixon: Maybe we can't even do that.

Dean: That's right. It's a real problem as to whether we could even do it. Plus there's a real problem in raising money. Uh, Mitchell has been working on raising some money. Uh, feeling he's got, you know, he's got one, he's one of the ones with the most to lose. Uh, but there's no denying the fact that the White House, and uh, Ehrlichman, Haldeman, Dean are involved in some of the early money decisions.

Nixon: How much money do you need?

Dean: I would say these people are going to cost, uh, a million dollars over the next, uh, two years. [*pause*]

President: We could get that.

Dean: Uh, huh.

Nixon: You, on the money, if you need the money, I mean, uh, you could get the money. Let's say—

Dean: Well, I think that we're going—

Nixon: What I mean is, you could, you could get a million dollars. And you could get it in cash. I, I know where it could be gotten.

Dean: Uh, huh. . . .

———

[Discussing perjury and the potential for indictments]

Dean: Well, here, what really, what really bothers me is that this, this growing situation—as I say it is growing because of the, the continued need to provide support for the . . . Watergate people who are going to . . . hold us up for everything they've got.

Nixon: That's right.

Dean: . . . and the need for some people to perjure themselves as they go down the road here. Uh, if this thing ever blows, and we're in a cover-up situation, I think it'd be extremely damaging to you.

Nixon: Sure. . . . The whole concept of Administration justice. . . .

Dean: That's what really troubles me. For example, what happens if it starts breaking, and they do find a criminal case against a Haldeman, a Dean, a Mitchell, an Ehrlichman? . . .

Nixon: Well, if it really comes down to that, we cannot, maybe—we'd have to shed it in order to contain it again.

Dean: That's right. I'm coming down to the—what I really think is that, that, Bob and John and John Mitchell and I should sit down and spend a day, or however long, to figure out (1) how this can be carved away from you, so it does not damage you or the Presidency. 'Cause it just can't. And it's not something, it, you're not involved in it and it's something you shouldn't—

Nixon: That is true.

———

[Discussing the fallout from a potential grand jury investigation, as well as potential payments]

Dean: Ask for another grand jury. The way it should be done though, is a way that—for example: I think that we could avoid, uh, criminal liability for countless people and the ones that did get it, it could be minimal.

Nixon: How?

Dean: Well, I think by just thinking it all through first, as to how some people could be granted immunity, uh . . .

Nixon: Like Magruder?

Dean: Yeah—to come forward. Uh, but some people are going to have to go to jail. That's the long and short of it, also.

Nixon: Who? Let's talk about that.

Dean: All right. Uh, I think I could, for one.

Nixon: You go to jail?

Dean: That's right.

Nixon: Oh, hell no. I can't see how you can. But, I—no . . .

Dean: Well, because . . .

Nixon: I can't see how, that—let me say I can't see how a legal case could be made against you, J—, uh, John. . . . What would you go to jail on [*unintelligible*]?

Dean: The obstruc—, the obstruction of justice.

Nixon: The obstruction of justice?

Dean: That's the only one that bothers me.

Nixon: Well, I don't know. I think that one, I think that, I feel could be cut off at the bass. Maybe the obstruction of Justice . . . Tell me—talking about your obstruction of justice role, I don't see it. I can't see it. You're . . .

Dean: Well, I've been a con—, I have been a conduit for information on, on taking care of people out there who are guilty of crimes.

Nixon: Oh, you mean like the, uh, oh—the blackmail.

Dean: The blackmail. Right.

Nixon: Well, I wonder if that part of it can't be—I wonder if that doesn't—let me put it frankly: I wonder if that doesn't have to be continued?

Dean: [*clears throat*]

Nixon: Let me cut it this way, let us suppose that you get, you, you get the million bucks and you get the proper way to handle it, and you could hold that side.

Dean: Uh huh.

Nixon: It would seem to me that would be worthwhile.

* * *

[Discussing the blackmail]

Nixon: Coming back, though, to this. So you got that . . . the, uh, hanging over. Now. If, uh, you see if you let it hang there, the point is you could let all or only part—The point is, your feeling is that we just can't continue to, to pay the blackmail of these guys?

Dean: I think that's our greatest jeopardy.

Haldeman: Yeah.

Nixon: Now, let me tell you, it's . . . no problem, we could, we could get the money. There is no problem in that. We can't provide the clemency. The money can be provided. Mitchell could provide the way to deliver it. That could be done. See what I mean?

[Discussing the risk to the presidency]

Nixon: All right. If you hunker down and fight it, fight it and what happens?

Dean: Your—

Nixon: Your view is that, that is, is not really a viable option.

Dean: It's a very, it's a high risk. A very high risk.

Nixon: A high risk, because your view is that what will happen out of that is that it's going to come out. Somebody's—Hunt—something's going to break loose—

Dean: Something is going to break and—

Nixon: When it breaks it'll look like the President—

Dean: —is covering up . . .

Haldeman: John's point is exactly right, that the erosion here now is going to you, and that is the thing that we've got to turn off, at whatever the cost and we've got to figure out where to turn it off at the lowest cost we can, but at whatever cost it takes.

Dean: That's what, that's what we have to do.

Nixon: Well, the erosion is inevitably going to come here, apart from anything, you know, people saying that, uh', well, the Watergate isn't a major concern. It isn't. But it would, but it will be. It's bound to be.

Dean: We cannot let you be tarnished by that situation.

Nixon: Well, [*unintelligible*] also because I—Although Ron Ziegler has to go out—They blame the [*unintelligible*] on the White House [*unintelligible*].

Dean: That's right.

Nixon: We don't, uh, uh, I say that the White House can't do it. Right?

Haldeman: Yeah.

Dean: Yes, sir.

"The Amenability of the President, Vice President, and Other Civil Officers to Federal Criminal Prosecution While in Office," by the Office of Legal Counsel (September 24, 1973)

The Office of Legal Counsel (OLC), established in 1934, is a group within the Department of Justice tasked with giving legal advice to the president and executive branch, including on the constitutionality of laws and executive actions. In 1973, as Nixon came under fire for the Watergate scandal, the threat of impeachment loomed, but so did the question of whether he would go to jail for his role in paying off the burglars and covering up the DNC break-in. Facing the question of whether a sitting president could be criminally indicted, Nixon's OLC wrote the memo excerpted here. The memo concludes that the president plays a unique role in the constitutional system that makes indictment inappropriate. Impeachment, not indictment, argues the memo, is the proper method for addressing presidential wrongdoing.

. . . II. IS THE PRESIDENT AMENABLE TO CRIMINAL PROCEEDINGS WHILE IN OFFICE?

This part of the memorandum deals with the question whether and to what extent the President is immune from criminal prosecution while he is in office. It has been suggested in the preceding part that Article I, sec. 3, clause 7 of the Constitution does not require the exhaustion of the impeachment process before an officer of the United States can be subjected to criminal proceedings. . . .

The difficulty of developing clear rules regarding the various possible facets of Presidential immunity is demonstrated by the limited and ambivalent case law developed in the fields of the amenability . . . of the President to civil litigation and to the judicial subpoena power. . . .

In the Burr treason trial, Chief Justice Marshall at first concluded that since the President is the first magistrate of the United States, and not a King who can do no wrong, he was subject to the judicial subpoena power. . . . In the Burr misdemeanor trial, however, which took place only a few months later, the Chief Justice had to qualify significantly his claim of the subpoena power over the President by conceding that the courts are not required "to proceed against the President as against an ordinary individual." . . .

Marshall's recognition of the special character of the Presidential office was expanded in Kendall v United States ex rel. Stokes, where the Court seemed to deny that it had any jurisdiction over the President: "The executive power is vested in a president; and so far as his powers are derived from the constitution, he is beyond the reach of any other department, except in the mode prescribed by the constitution through the impeachment."

It is significant that this apparent total disclaimer of any judicial authority over the President also was qualified by adding the clause "so far as his powers are derived from the constitution." . . .

. . . It appears that under our constitutional plan it cannot be said either that the courts have the same jurisdiction over the President as if he were an ordinary citizen or that the President is absolutely immune from the jurisdiction of the courts in regard to any kind of claim. The proper approach is to find the proper balance between the normal functions of the courts and the special responsibilities and functions of the Presidency. . . .

2. Would criminal proceedings against a President be ineffective and inappropriate because of his powers regarding (a) prosecution, (b) Executive privilege, and (c) pardons?

The Presidency, however, creates a special situation in view of the control of all criminal proceedings by the Attorney General who serves at the pleasure and normally subject to the direction of the President and the pardoning power vested in the President. . . . Hence, it could be argued that a President's status as defendant in a criminal case would be repugnant to his office of Chief Executive, which includes the power to oversee prosecutions. In other words, just as a person cannot be judge in his own case, he cannot be prosecutor and defendant at the same time. . . .

Further, the problem of Executive privilege may create the appearance of so serious a conflict of interest as to make it appear improper that the President should be a defendant in a criminal case. . . .

3. Would criminal proceedings unduly interfere in a direct or formal sense with the conduct of the presidency? . . .

A necessity to defend a criminal trial and to attend court in connection with it . . . would interfere with the President's unique official duties, most of which cannot be performed by anyone else. It might be suggested that the same is true with the defense of impeachment proceedings; but this is a risk expressly contemplated by the Constitution and is a necessary incident of the impeachment process. The Constitutional Convention was aware of this problem but rejected a proposal that the President should be suspended upon impeachment by the House until acquitted by the Senate.

During the past century, the duties of the Presidency, however, have become so onerous that a President may not be able fully to discharge the powers and duties of his office if he had to defend a criminal prosecution. . . .

This would suggest strongly that in view of the unique aspects of the office of the President, criminal proceedings against a President in office should not go beyond a point where they could result in so serious a physical interference with the President's performance of his official duties that it would amount to an incapacitation. . . .

4. Would initiation or prosecution of criminal proceedings, as a practical matter, unduly impede the power to govern, and also be inappropriate, prior to impeachment because of the symbolic significance of the Presidency? . . .

This may be an overstatement but surely it contains a kernel of truth, namely that the President is the symbolic head of the Nation. To wound him by a criminal proceeding is to hamstring the operation of the whole governmental apparatus, both in foreign and domestic affairs. It is not to be forgotten that the modern Presidency, under whatever party, has had to assume a leadership role undreamed of in the eighteenth and early nineteenth centuries. The spectacle of an indicted President still trying to serve as Chief Executive boggles the imagination.

Would it not be incongruous to bring him down, before the

Congress has acted, by a jury of twelve, selected by chance "off the street" as Holmes put it? Surely the House and Senate, via impeachment, are more appropriate agencies for such a crucial task, made unavoidably political by the nature of the "defendant." . . .

A President who would face jury trial rather than resign could be expected to persist to the point of appealing an adverse verdict. The process could then drag out for months. By contrast the authorized process of impeachment is well adapted to achieving a relatively speedy and final resolution by a nation based Senate trial. The whole country is represented at the trial, there is no appeal from the verdict, and removal opens the way for placing the political system on a new and more healthy foundation. . . .

A further factor relevant here is the President's role as guardian and executor of the four year popular mandate expressed in the most recent balloting for the Presidency. Under our developed constitutional order, the presidential election is the only national election, and there is no effective substitute for it. . . . Because only the President can receive and continuously discharge the popular mandate expressed quadrennially in the presidential election, an interruption would be political and constitutionally a traumatic event. . . .

In suggesting that an impeachment proceeding is the only appropriate way to deal with a president while in office we realize that there are certain drawbacks such as the running of a statute of limitations while the President is in office, thus preventing any trial for such offenses. In this difficult area all courses of action have costs and we recognize that a situation of the type just mentioned could cause a complete hiatus in criminal liability. We doubt, however, that this gap in the law is sufficient to overcome the arguments against subjecting a President to indictment and criminal trial while in office.

"Attached Memorandum to Leon Jaworski," by Carl B. Feldbaum et al. (February 12, 1974)

On November 1, 1973, Leon Jaworski was appointed as the new special prosecutor charged with investigating the Watergate scandal. Though the special prosecutor's office was located within the Department of Justice, Jaworski was fiercely independent. He knew Nixon would not get away with shutting him down after the debacle of the Saturday Night Massacre. Here, a staffer in Jaworski's office voices an argument at odds with the OLC's. Nixon, like any other individual, he writes, must be subject to indictment, so everyone stands equal before the law. If the special prosecutor's team finds that Nixon broke the law, this memo argues they must say so.

RECOMMENDATION FOR ACTION BY THE WATERGATE GRAND JURY

I.

. . . No principles are more firmly rooted in our traditions, or more at stake in the decision facing this office and the Grand Jury, than that there shall be equal justice for all and that "(n)o

man in this country is so high that he is above the law." . . .
For us or the grand jury to shirk from an appropriate expression of our honest assessment of the evidence of the President's
guilt would not only be a departure from our responsibilities
but a dangerous precedent damaging to the rule of law. The inevitable conclusion would be that one man, at least, is so far
different from anybody else as to be above the ordinary processes of the criminal law. The implications of such a conclusion would be unfortunate under ordinary circumstances; but
we are not faced with ordinary circumstances—we are dealing
with the very man in whom the Constitution reposes not only
the most power in our society but also the highest and final obligation to ensure that the law is obeyed and enforced. Thus,
failure to deal evenhandedly with the President would be an
affront to the very principle on which our system is built. . . .
The result would probably be greater public disrespect for the
integrity of the legal process than has already been created by
public knowledge of attempts by the nation's highest officials
to put themselves beyond the law.

It follows from this analysis of our responsibilities and
those of the grand jury that our duty is to make a recommen-
dation with respect to the President which is directed toward
enforcement of the criminal law. The existence of the impeachment mechanism in no way alters this conclusion. Impeachment
is an avowedly "political" process by which the people's
representatives can remove a sitting President before the
end of his term based on a "political" judgment about his
fitness to govern. . . . In contrast, our criminal justice process
exists, and is universally perceived to exist, for a different purpose, entailing a different standard: to prosecute crimes with
reference to an apolitical code applied objectively to all citizens. For this very reason our office was created as an office of
criminal prosecution, not (as it might have been) as an independent commission to determine all the facts and then to

make recommendations about anyone's fitness to continue to serve in public office. . . .

The constitutional allocation of these separate functions means that to let "political" considerations of the kind now being debated in Congress intrude upon the decision-making of this office and of the Grand Jury would be to confuse the functions of law enforcement and of impeachment, and the result would be further to undermine public confidence in the integrity of the legal process. . . .

Thus, we believe that it would be impermissible for this office to determine its course of action on the basis of a belief that the President should or should not be removed from public office. By the same token, we cannot responsibly leave the question of the President's criminal guilt or innocence to the "political" process and the "political" judgment of impeachment. To do so, we feel, would be an abdication of our duties and those of the Grand Jury, premised only on the view that for the most powerful official in the country, the essence of "justice" is limited to the decision of his fitness to govern and to ouster from office if he is found wanting. The Constitution itself decries such a premise by stating that a person convicted after impeachment "shall nevertheless be liable and subject to Indictment, Trial, Judgment and Punishment according to Law." If the President were placed so much apart from all other citizens that he could even escape the determination of whether there is probable cause to believe that he has committed a crime, one can only imagine how much greater the public cynicism would be. . . .

II . . .

The other serious argument against indictment is that it would be the "equivalent" of impeachment because if the President were convicted and incarcerated (and even if he had to prepare for and undergo trial) he would no longer be able to discharge the duties of his office; and in any event the country would be brought to a standstill prior to trial by the existence of outstanding and unresolved charges against a President who refused to resign or was not impeached.

The answer to this argument is that the disruption caused by indictment and trial of the President would be no greater, and possibly less, than that caused by the impeachment process. . . .

. . . The fact that some evidence of criminal activity will probably become public in any event also means the public will eventually realize we had evidence we did not act upon. This would certainly raise serious questions about the performance of this office and the integrity of the criminal justice system.

Finally, the Framers obviously contemplated some disruption in the Executive Branch as a necessary and bearable cost to providing the people—through the impeachment mechanism—with a remedy for gross misconduct. . . .

In sum, if the Grand Jury finds probable cause to believe the President acted criminally, then it is essential that this simple, primary truth emerge from the action we and the Grand Jury take: that but for the fact that he is President, Richard Nixon would have been indicted.

"Speech on the Nixon Articles of Impeachment," by Barbara Charline Jordan (July 25, 1974)

In 1972, Barbara Charline Jordan of Texas became the first Southern African American woman elected to the House of Representatives. She held a coveted seat on the House Judiciary Committee, the panel running the impeachment inquiry into Richard Nixon. Much of the inquiry focused on Nixon's reported violations of criminal laws. But Barbara Jordan, in this now-famous opening statement, analyzed Nixon's wrongdoing within the broader values of the Constitution. To Jordan, that document was a source of inspiration, a testament to America's continued attempts to realize its democratic values. What was at stake in her role as "inquisitor" was not just the conviction of one powerful man—it was the fate of our constitutional system.

Thank you, Mr. Chairman.

Mr. Chairman, I join my colleague Mr. Rangel in thanking you for giving the junior members of this committee the glorious opportunity of sharing the pain of this inquiry. Mr. Chairman, you are a strong man, and it has not been easy but we have tried as best we can to give you as much assistance as possible.

Earlier today, we heard the beginning of the Preamble to the Constitution of the United States: "We, the people." It's a very eloquent beginning. But when that document was completed on the seventeenth of September in 1787, I was not included in that "We, the people." I felt somehow for many years that George Washington and Alexander Hamilton just left me out by mistake. But through the process of amendment, interpretation, and court decision, I have finally been included in "We, the people."

Today I am an inquisitor. An hyperbole would not be fictional and would not overstate the solemnness that I feel right now. My faith in the Constitution is whole, it is complete, it is total. And I am not going to sit here and be an idle spectator to the diminution, the subversion, the destruction, of the Constitution.

"Who can so properly be the inquisitors for the nation as the representatives of the nation themselves?" "The subjects of its jurisdiction are those offenses which proceed from the misconduct of public men." And that's what we're talking about. In other words, [the jurisdiction comes] from the abuse or violation of some public trust . . . It is a misreading of the Constitution, for any member here to assert that for a member to vote for an article of impeachment means that that member must be convinced that the President should be removed from office.

The Constitution doesn't say that. The powers relating to impeachment are an essential check in the hands of the body of the Legislature against and upon the encroachments of the Executive. The division between the two branches of the Legislature, the House and the Senate, assigning to the one the right to accuse and to the other the right to judge, the Framers of this Constitution were very astute. They did not make the accusers and the judgers—and the judges the same person.

We know the nature of impeachment. We've been talking about it awhile now. It is chiefly designed for the President and his high ministers to somehow be called into account. It is designed to "bridle" the Executive if he engages in excesses. . . . The Framers confided in the Congress the power, if need be, to remove the President in order to strike a delicate balance between a President swollen with power and grown tyrannical and preservation of the independence of the Executive.

The nature of impeachment: a narrowly channeled exception to the separation-of-powers maxim. The Federal Convention of 1787 said that. It limited impeachment to high crimes and misdemeanors and discounted and opposed the term "maladministration." "It is to be used only for great misdemeanors," so it was said in the North Carolina ratification convention. And in the Virginia ratification convention: "We do not trust our liberty to a particular branch. We need one branch to check the others." . . .

The drawing of political lines goes to the motivation behind impeachment; but impeachment must proceed within the confines of the constitutional term "high crime[s] and misdemeanors." . . .

Common sense would be revolted if we engaged upon this process for petty reasons. Congress has a lot to do: Appropriations, Tax Reform, Health Insurance, Campaign Finance Reform, Housing, Environmental Protection, Energy Sufficiency, Mass Transportation. Pettiness cannot be allowed to stand in the face of such overwhelming problems. So today we are not being petty. We are trying to be big, because the task we have before us is a big one. . . .

We were further cautioned today that perhaps these proceedings ought to be delayed because certainly there would be new evidence forthcoming from the President of the United

States. There has not even been an obfuscated indication that this committee would receive any additional materials from the President. The committee subpoena is outstanding, and if the President wants to supply that material, the committee sits here. The fact is that on yesterday, the American people waited with great anxiety for eight hours, not knowing whether their President would obey an order of the Supreme Court of the United States.

At this point, I would like to juxtapose a few of the impeachment criteria with some of the actions the President has engaged in. Impeachment criteria: James Madison, from the Virginia ratification convention. "If the President be connected in any suspicious manner with any person and there be grounds to believe that he will shelter him, he may be impeached."

We have heard time and time again that the evidence reflects the payment to defendants money. The President had knowledge that these funds were being paid and these were funds collected for the 1972 presidential campaign. We know that the President met with Mr. Henry Petersen twenty-seven times to discuss matters related to Watergate, and immediately thereafter met with the very persons who were implicated in the information Mr. Petersen was receiving. The words are: "If the President is connected in any suspicious manner with any person and there be grounds to believe that he will shelter that person, he may be impeached."

Justice Story: "Impeachment . . . is intended for occasional and extraordinary cases where a superior power acting for the whole people is put into operation to protect their rights and rescue their liberties from violations." We know about the Huston plan. We know about the break-in of the psychiatrist's office. We know that there was absolute complete direction on September 3rd when the President indicated that a surreptitious entry had been made in Dr. Fielding's office, after having met with Mr. Ehrlichman and Mr. Young. "Protect their rights." "Rescue their liberties from violation."

The Carolina ratification convention impeachment criteria: those are impeachable "who behave amiss or betray their public trust." Beginning shortly after the Watergate break-in and continuing to the present time, the President has engaged in a series of public statements and actions designed to thwart the lawful investigation by government prosecutors. Moreover, the President has made public announcements and assertions bearing on the Watergate case, which the evidence will show he knew to be false. These assertions, false assertions, impeachable, those who misbehave. Those who "behave amiss or betray the public trust."

James Madison again at the Constitutional Convention: "A President is impeachable if he attempts to subvert the Constitution." The Constitution charges the President with the task of taking care that the laws be faithfully executed, and yet the President has counseled his aides to commit perjury, willfully disregard the secrecy of grand jury proceedings, conceal surreptitious entry, attempt to compromise a federal judge, while publicly displaying his cooperation with the processes of criminal justice. "A President is impeachable if he attempts to subvert the Constitution."

If the impeachment provision in the Constitution of the United States will not reach the offenses charged here, then perhaps that eighteenth-century Constitution should be abandoned to a twentieth-century paper shredder!

Has the President committed offenses, and planned, and directed, and acquiesced in a course of conduct which the Constitution will not tolerate? That's the question. We know that. We know the question. We should now forthwith proceed to answer the question. It is reason, and not passion, which must guide our deliberations, guide our debate, and guide our decision.

Mr. Chairman, I yield back the balance of my time.

Articles of Impeachment
Against Richard Nixon
(July 27–30, 1974)

The House Judiciary Committee, along with the Senate Watergate Committee, gathered explosive testimony and information from 1973 through 1974. Their work revealed that President Nixon had personally been involved in the cover-up of the Watergate break-in, obstructing justice and attempting to interfere in the 1972 election. At first the committee members' views were split by party, with most Republicans opposing impeachment. But after the testimony of Dean and others, a small number of Republicans defected to support impeachment. Three articles of impeachment were ultimately passed by the Judiciary Committee. The first two passed 27–11, with unanimous support among Democrats, with six of the Committee's seventeen Republican members joining them. The third article passed 21–17, with two Democrats defecting and only two Republicans voting in favor. Putting country above party, Republican Robert McClory, a yes vote on two of the articles of impeachment, urged his fellow congressman to "speak in terms of the Constitution" in order to make the impeachment "a guide for future presidents." Two other articles, on Nixon's bombing of Cambodia and underpayment of income taxes, were rejected by the Judiciary Committee by 26–12 votes.

ARTICLE 1

In his conduct of the office of President of the United States, Richard M. Nixon, in violation of his constitutional oath faithfully to execute the office of President of the United States and, to the best of his ability, preserve, protect, and defend the Constitution of the United States, and in violation of his constitutional duty to take care that the laws be faithfully executed, has prevented, obstructed, and impeded the administration of justice, in that:

On June 17, 1972, and prior thereto, agents of the Committee for the Re-election of the President committed unlawful entry of the headquarters of the Democratic National Committee in Washington, District of Columbia, for the purpose of securing political intelligence. Subsequent thereto, Richard M. Nixon, using the powers of his high office, engaged personally and through his close subordinates and agents, in a course of conduct or plan designed to delay, impede, and obstruct the investigation of such illegal entry; to cover up, conceal and protect those responsible; and to conceal the existence and scope of other unlawful covert activities.

The means used to implement this course of conduct or plan included one or more of the following:

1. making false or misleading statements to lawfully authorized investigative officers and employees of the United States;
2. withholding relevant and material evidence or information from lawfully authorized investigative officers and employees of the United States;

3. approving, condoning, acquiescing in, and counselling witnesses with respect to the giving of false or misleading statements to lawfully authorized investigative officers . . .
4. interfering or endeavouring to interfere with the conduct of investigations . . .
5. approving, condoning, and acquiescing in, the surreptitious payment of substantial sums of money for the purpose of obtaining the silence or influencing the testimony of witnesses . . .
6. endeavouring to misuse the Central Intelligence Agency, an agency of the United States;
7. disseminating information received from officers of the Department of Justice of the United States . . . for the purpose of aiding and assisting such subjects in their attempts to avoid criminal liability;
8. making or causing to be made false or misleading public statements for the purpose of deceiving the people of the United States into believing that a thorough and complete investigation had been conducted with respect to allegations of misconduct on the part of personnel of the executive branch . . . and that there was no involvement of such personnel in such misconduct: or
9. endeavouring to cause prospective defendants, and individuals duly tried and convicted, to expect favoured treatment and consideration in return for their silence or false testimony . . .

In all of this, Richard M. Nixon has acted in a manner contrary to his trust as President and subversive of constitutional government, to the great prejudice of the cause of law and justice and to the manifest injury of the people of the United States. . . .

ARTICLE 2

Using the powers of the office of President of the United States, Richard M. Nixon . . . has repeatedly engaged in conduct violating the constitutional rights of citizens, impairing the due and proper administration of justice and the conduct of lawful inquiries, or contravening the laws governing agencies of the executive branch and the purposed of these agencies.

This conduct has included one or more of the following:

1. He has . . . endeavoured to obtain from the Internal Revenue Service . . . confidential information contained in income tax returns for purposed not authorized by law . . .
2. He misused the Federal Bureau of Investigation, the Secret Service, and other executive personnel . . . by directing or authorizing such agencies or personnel to conduct or continue electronic surveillance or other investigations for purposes unrelated to national security, the enforcement of laws, or any other lawful function of his office . . .
3. He has . . . authorized and permitted to be maintained a secret investigative unit within the office of the President . . . which unlawfully utilized the resources of the Central Intelligence Agency, engaged in covert and unlawful activities, and attempted to prejudice the constitutional right of an accused to a fair trial.
4. He has failed to take care that the laws were faithfully executed by failing to act when he knew or had reason to know that his close subordinates endeavoured to impede and frustrate lawful inquiries . . .
5. In disregard of the rule of law, he knowingly misused the executive power by interfering with agencies of the exec-

utive branch . . . in violation of his duty to take care that
the laws be faithfully executed . . .

ARTICLE 3

In his conduct of the office of President of the United States,
Richard M. Nixon . . . has failed without lawful cause or excuse
to produce papers and things as directed by duly authorized
subpoenas issued by the Committee on the Judiciary . . . and
willfully disobeyed such subpoenas. . . . In refusing to produce
these papers and things Richard M. Nixon, substituting his
judgment as to what materials were necessary for the inquiry,
interposed the powers of the Presidency against the lawful
subpoenas of the House of Representatives, thereby assuming
to himself functions and judgments necessary to the exercise
of the sole power of impeachment vested by the Constitution
in the House of Representatives.

"Address Announcing Resignation," by Richard Nixon (August 8, 1974)

President Richard Nixon was never formally impeached. The Judiciary Committee voted on the articles of impeachment, but the full House of Representatives never had a chance to vote. Days before the Judiciary Committee voted, Nixon was forced by the Supreme Court to release the tapes from the secret recording device he had set up in the Oval Office. The damning evidence from the tapes turned many of his most steadfast Republican supporters against him. Senator Barry Goldwater led a delegation to the White House, saying Nixon might get as few as four votes in support if the impeachment trial came to the Senate. Facing immense political pressure and assured of defeat, on August 8, 1974, Nixon became the first and only president to resign from office, announcing his decision in this nationally televised speech.

Good evening. This is the thirty-seventh time I have spoken to you from this office, where so many decisions have been made that shaped the history of this Nation. Each time I have done so to discuss with you some matter that I believe affected the national interest.

In all the decisions I have made in my public life, I have always tried to do what was best for the Nation. Throughout the long and difficult period of Watergate, I have felt it was my duty to persevere, to make every possible effort to complete the term of office to which you elected me.

In the past few days, however, it has become evident to me that I no longer have a strong enough political base in the Congress to justify continuing that effort. As long as there was such a base, I felt strongly that it was necessary to see the constitutional process through to its conclusion, that to do otherwise would be unfaithful to the spirit of that deliberately difficult process and a dangerously destabilizing precedent for the future.

But with the disappearance of that base, I now believe that the constitutional purpose has been served, and there is no longer a need for the process to be prolonged.

I would have preferred to carry through to the finish whatever the personal agony it would have involved, and my family unanimously urged me to do so. But the interest of the Nation must always come before any personal considerations.

From the discussions I have had with Congressional and other leaders, I have concluded that because of the Watergate matter I might not have the support of the Congress that I would consider necessary to back the very difficult decisions and carry out the duties of this office in the way the interests of the Nation would require.

I have never been a quitter. To leave office before my term is completed is abhorrent to every instinct in my body. But as President, I must put the interest of America first. America needs a full-time President and a full-time Congress, particularly at this time with problems we face at home and abroad.

To continue to fight through the months ahead for my personal vindication would almost totally absorb the time and attention of both the President and the Congress in a period when our entire focus should be on the great issues of peace abroad and prosperity without inflation at home.

Therefore, I shall resign the Presidency effective at noon tomorrow. Vice President Ford will be sworn in as President at that hour in this office.

As I recall the high hopes for America with which we began this second term, I feel a great sadness that I will not be here in this office working on your behalf to achieve those hopes in the next two and a half years. But in turning over direction of the Government to Vice President Ford, I know, as I told the Nation when I nominated him for that office ten months ago, that the leadership of America will be in good hands. . . .

By taking this action, I hope that I will have hastened the start of that process of healing which is so desperately needed in America.

I regret deeply any injuries that may have been done in the course of the events that led to this decision. I would say only that if some of my Judgments were wrong, and some were wrong, they were made in what I believed at the time to be the best interest of the Nation. . . .

I shall leave this office with regret at not completing my term, but with gratitude for the privilege of serving as your President for the past five and a half years. These years have been a momentous time in the history of our Nation and the world. They have been a time of achievement in which we can all be proud, achievements that represent the shared efforts of the Administration, the Congress, and the people. . . .

For more than a quarter of a century in public life I have shared in the turbulent history of this era. I have fought for what I believed in. I have tried to the best of my ability to discharge those duties and meet those responsibilities that were entrusted to me. . . .

When I first took the oath of office as President five and a half years ago, I made this sacred commitment, to "consecrate my office, my energies, and all the wisdom I can summon to the cause of peace among nations."

I have done my very best in all the days since to be true to that pledge. As a result of these efforts, I am confident that the world is a safer place today, not only for the people of America but for the people of all nations, and that all of our children have a better chance than before of living in peace rather than dying in war.

This, more than anything, is what I hoped to achieve when I sought the Presidency. This, more than anything, is what I hope will be my legacy to you, to our country, as I leave the Presidency.

To have served in this office is to have felt a very personal sense of kinship with each and every American. In leaving it, I do so with this prayer: May God's grace be with you in all the days ahead.

"Granting a Pardon
to Richard Nixon,"
by Gerald Ford
(September 8, 1974)

When Richard Nixon resigned, his vice president Gerald Ford was first in line to occupy the presidential office. Now in office, President Ford faced a situation unprecedented in American history: how should he address the controversy surrounding a former president who had been credibly accused of crimes and forced out of office? Ford's decision proved famously controversial: he issued a pardon to Richard Nixon of all potential crimes, in an effort to heal the country's political divides. This decision assured that Nixon would never face criminal charges for his role in Watergate. Ford's pardon became a defining feature of his brief presidency.

Richard Nixon became the thirty-seventh President of the United States on January 20, 1969 and was reelected in 1972 for a second term by the electors of forty-nine of the fifty states. His term in office continued until his resignation on August 9, 1974.

Pursuant to resolutions of the House of Representatives, its Committee on the Judiciary conducted an inquiry and investigation on the impeachment of the President extending over more than eight months. The hearings of the Committee and its deliberations, which received wide national publicity over television, radio, and in printed media, resulted in votes adverse to Richard Nixon on recommended Articles of Impeachment.

As a result of certain acts or omissions occurring before his resignation from the Office of President, Richard Nixon has become liable to possible indictment and trial for offenses against the United States. Whether or not he shall be so prosecuted depends on findings of the appropriate grand jury and on the discretion of the authorized prosecutor. Should an indictment ensue, the accused shall then be entitled to a fair trial by an impartial jury, as guaranteed to every individual by the Constitution.

It is believed that a trial of Richard Nixon, if it became necessary, could not fairly begin until a year or more has elapsed. In the meantime, the tranquility to which this nation has been restored by the events of recent weeks could be irreparably lost by the prospects of bringing to trial a former President of the United States. The prospects of such trial will cause prolonged and divisive debate over the propriety of exposing to further punishment and degradation a man who has already paid the unprecedented penalty of relinquishing the highest elective office of the United States.

Now, THEREFORE, I, GERALD R. FORD, President of the United States, pursuant to the pardon power conferred upon me by Article II, Section 2, of the Constitution, have granted and by these presents do grant a full, free, and absolute pardon unto Richard Nixon for all offenses against the United States which he, Richard Nixon, has committed or may have committed or taken part in during the period from January 20, 1969 through August 9, 1974.

IN WITNESS WHEREOF, I have hereunto set my hand this eighth day of September, in the year of our Lord nineteen hundred and seventy-four, and of the Independence of the United States of America the one hundred and ninety-ninth.

Part IV

BILL CLINTON

"To Kenneth W. Starr, Re: Indictability of the President," by Ronald Rotunda (May 13, 1998)

President Bill Clinton was mired in scandal practically from the moment he took office in 1993. In 1994, Congress appointed Ken Starr to investigate Clinton's financial dealings in a controversy that was known as Whitewater. Starr was appointed under the Ethics in Government Act, a law President Jimmy Carter signed after the Watergate affair that ensured the prosecutor greater independence from the executive branch. With this broad protection and with the authorization of Attorney General Janet Reno, Starr expanded his investigation into Clinton's sexual relationship with White House intern and staffer Monica Lewinsky. Starr thought Clinton might have committed perjury and obstruction of justice. But the Nixon-era 1973 OLC memo said a president could not be indicted while in office. So Starr asked his advisor Ronald Rotunda, a prominent attorney and former Watergate investigator, to assess whether the OLC memo was correct that a president could not be indicted under the Constitution.

In this memo, not released to the public until 2017, Rotunda argues that since no one can be above the law under the Constitution, the president must be subject to

> *indictment. Starr, however, declined to act on Rotunda's advice, ultimately declining to pursue indictment in favor of giving information over to Congress for use in a potential impeachment.*

Dear Judge Starr:

You have asked my legal opinion as to whether a sitting President is subject to indictment. Does the Constitution immunize a President from being indicted for criminal activities while serving in the office of President? . . . In short, is a sitting President above the criminal law?

As this opinion letter makes clear, I conclude that, in the circumstances of this case, President Clinton is subject to indictment and criminal prosecution, although it may be the case that he could not be imprisoned (assuming that he is convicted and that imprisonment is the appropriate punishment) until after he leaves that office. . . .

In this country, the U.S. Supreme Court has repeatedly reaffirmed the state that no one is "above the law." The Constitution grants no one immunity from the criminal laws. . . .

As the judiciary has noted in the past, the President "does not embody the nation's sovereignty. He is not above the law's commands. . . ." The people "do not forfeit through elections the right to have the law construed against and applied to every citizen. Nor does the Impeachment Clause imply immunity from routine court process."

. . . As discussed in detail below, if the Constitution really provides that the President must be impeached before he can be prosecuted for breaking the criminal law even if the President commits a crime prior to the time he became President, or if he commits a crime in his personal capacity, not in his official capacity as President, our Constitution has created serious anomalies.

First, it is quite clear that a President may be impeached for actions that do not violate any criminal statute. Acts that (a) constitute impeachable offenses and (b) are violations of a crime created by statute (our Constitution recognizes no common law crimes) are two different categories of acts. Moreover, if the President does commit a crime, that does not necessarily mean that he must be impeached, because some crimes do not merit impeachment and removal from office. . . . If there is no recourse against the President, if he cannot be prosecuted for violating the criminal laws, he will be above the law. . . .

. . . If the Constitution prevents the President from being indicted for violations of one or more federal criminal statutes, even if those statutory violations are not impeachable offences, then the Constitution authorizes the President to be above the law. But the Constitution creates an Executive Branch with the President under a sworn obligation to faithfully executive the law. The Constitution does not create an absolute Monarch above the law. . . .

. . . The question is not, as an abstract matter, whether any sitting President is immune from the criminal laws of the state or federal governments as long as he is in office. Rather, the question is whether given the enactment of the Independent Counsel law under which the OIC operates, given the historical background that led to that law, and given the constitutionality of that law as determined by Morrison v. Olson it is constitutional for a grand jury to indict this President if the evidence demonstrates beyond a reasonable doubt that the President is part of an extensive and continuing conspiracy, stretching over many years, involving witness tampering, document destruction, perjury, subornation of perjury, obstruction of justice, and illegal pay-offs all serious allegations that in no way relate to the President Clinton's official duties, even though some of the alleged violations occurred after he became President. . . .

THE STRUCTURE AND LANGUAGE OF THE UNITED STATES CONSTITUTION

Chief Justice Marshall explained that the Constitution "assigns to different departments their respective powers." So that "those limits may not be mistaken or forgotten, the constitution is written. . . ."

Because we live under a *written* constitution, and the Constitution was written so that we would be governed by the written words, it is useful to look at what that writing says about immunities from prosecution. Let us look at the language of the Constitution.

Our written Constitution has two specific sections that refer to what may be categorized as some type of "immunity" from the ordinary reach of the laws.

THE PRIVILEGE FROM ARREST

First, Senators and Representatives are "privileged from Arrest during their Attendance at the Session of their respective Houses, and in going to and returning from the same . . ." except in cases of "Treason, Felony and Breach of the Peace. . . ."

. . . The Framers of our Constitution thought about immunity, and when they did, they gave a limited immunity to the Senators and Representatives. No similar clause applies to any member of the Executive Branch nor any member of the Judicial Branch. . . .

THE SPEECH OR DEBATE CLAUSE

The same clause of the Constitution contains the only other reference to a privilege or immunity from the criminal law. It provides that, "for any Speech or Debate in either House, they shall not be questioned in any other Place." . . .

. . . [T]he Speech or Debate Privilege, like the Arrest Privilege, only applies to the legislative branch, not the executive branch. The Constitutional language makes that quite clear. The existence of these two privileges and the absence of any similarly clear language creating any sort of Presidential privilege is significant. If the Framers of our Constitution had wanted to create some constitutional privilege to shield the President or any other member of the Executive Branch from criminal indictment (or to prevent certain officials from being indicted before they were impeached), they could have drafted such a privilege. They certainly know how to draft immunity language, for they drafted a very limited immunity for the federal legislature.

Yet, even in the case of federal legislators, the Constitution gives no immunity from indictment. . . .

THE IMPEACHMENT CLAUSE

The Language

There is only one impeachment clause in the Constitution. It does not purport to distinguish the impeachment of a federal judge from the Vice President, nor does it distinguish the impeachment of the Vice President from the President. The clause provides:

> "Judgment in Cases of Impeachment shall not extend further than to removal from Office, and disqualification to hold and enjoy any Office of honor, Trust, or Profit under the United States: but the Party convicted shall nevertheless be liable and subject to Indictment, Trial, Judgment, and Punishment, according to Law."

This clause indicates that Congress should not be entrusted with the power to impose any penalty on an impeached official other than (or no greater than) removal from office and disqualification from further office. Criminal penalties would be left to the judiciary. . . . The clause does not state that criminal prosecution must come after an impeachment, nor does it state that the refusal of the House to impeach (or the Senate to remove from office) would bar a subsequent criminal prosecution. . . .

Of course, impeachment by the House and conviction by the Senate is the only constitutional way to remove the President or Vice President or federal judges from office. A criminal conviction in an Article III federal court of a federal official does not remove this official from office, even if the criminal act would also constitute "high crimes or misdemeanors." . . .

When those who argue that the President is immune from the criminal law until after he has been impeached look to the historical sources, the very most that they could draw from the historical debates in support of their view is that there certainly was no agreement to create any Presidential immunity from criminal indictment (either absolute or temporary), for the easiest way to create it (temporary or otherwise) would have been to add a clause to the Constitution defining its existence and extent. In fact, the contemporary sources suggest that the Constitution provides no criminal immunity for any President who commits crimes in his personal capacity.

This analysis should not be surprising; it is the same conclusion reached in Nixon v. Sirica, where the Court after examining the Constitutional debates and the views of the Framers of our Constitution said: "The Constitution makes no mention of special presidential immunities. Indeed, the Executive Branch generally is afforded none. This silence cannot be ascribed to oversight."

Later, this same Court said: "Lacking textual support, counsel for the President nonetheless would have us infer immunity from the President's political mandate, or from his vulnerability to impeachment, or from his broad discretionary powers. These are invitations to refashion the Constitution and we reject them." . . .

TEMPORARY IMMUNITY
CREATED BY STATUTE . . .

President Clinton, like President Nixon, may wish to argue that the Presidency is "unique," and that the President alone represents "the Executive Branch." Consequently, it is argued, the President alone is immune from the criminal laws while he is sitting as President.

The Court, in Nixon v. Sirica, explicitly rejected that argument. . . .

. . . If an official subject to impeachment (such as the President, Vice President, or a federal judge) could not be indicted until after he or she had been impeached, then Congress would control the decision whether to prosecute. But such a power would be inconsistent with the doctrine of separation of powers, which does not give Congress a role in the execution of the laws.

The decision to prosecute or not prosecute is a decision that cannot lie with the legislature. In the instant case, it lies with the Independent Counsel, who, under the statute, stands in the shoes of the Attorney General. The decision to appoint the Independent Counsel rests in the unreviewable discretion of the Attorney General. The U.S. Supreme Court has made clear that neither the courts nor Congress can require the appointment of an Independent Counsel.

The decision to indict a sitting President lies with the Grand Jury, not with the House of Representatives or Senate. . . .

These factors all buttress and lead to the same conclusion: it is proper, constitutional, and legal for a federal grand jury to indict a sitting President for serious criminal acts that are not part of, and are contrary to, the President's official duties. In this country, no one, even President Clinton, is above the law.

This conclusion does not imply that a President must be required to serve an actual prison term before he leaves office. The defendant President could remain free pending his trial, and the trial court could defer any prison sentence until he leaves office. . . .

Before or after indictment, Congress could exercise its independent judgment as to whether to begin impeachment proceedings or await the conclusion of the criminal proceedings. Or, if Congress did not wish to postpone the impeachment proceedings, Congress if it wished (and if the President agreed), could ask the Independent Counsel to delay the criminal trial. The President could also petition the court to stay or postpone the criminal trial until the impeachment proceedings were concluded.

Neither the criminal proceeding nor the impeachment proceeding will control the other. As Solicitor General Bork pointed out a quarter of a century ago: "Because the two processes have different objects, the considerations relevant to one may not be relevant to the other."

For that reason, neither conviction nor acquittal in one

trial, though it may be persuasive, need automatically determine the result in the other trial."

And, the House or Senate may conclude that "a particular offense, though properly punishable in the courts, did not warrant" either impeachment or removal from office.

Referral from Independent Counsel Kenneth W. Starr to the House Committee on the Judiciary (September 11, 1998)

Ken Starr, former U.S. solicitor general, was appointed as an independent counsel in 1994 under the Ethics in Government Act. His original mandate, per the three-judge panel that appointed him, was to investigate alleged financial wrongdoing by President Clinton in what was known as the Whitewater affair. But Starr's investigation later expanded to include President Clinton's actions during the Paula Jones sexual harassment lawsuit and the cover-up of an affair with former White House intern and staffer Monica Lewinsky. Starr wrote an exhaustive report on Clinton's transgressions. It is now famously remembered for its explicit sexual detail. But Starr's account was shared with Congress because he believed Clinton's actions may have constituted grounds for impeachment. Starr chose not to prosecute Clinton, but he did believe that Clinton committed perjury and obstruction of justice—acts that might warrant congressional punishment.

INTRODUCTION

As required by Section 595(c) of Title 28 of the United States Code, the Office of the Independent Counsel ("OIC" or "Office") hereby submits substantial and credible information that President William Jefferson Clinton committed acts that may constitute grounds for an impeachment.

The information reveals that President Clinton:

- lied under oath at a civil deposition while he was a defendant in a sexual harassment lawsuit;

- lied under oath to a grand jury;

- attempted to influence the testimony of a potential witness who had direct knowledge of facts that would reveal the falsity of his deposition testimony;

- attempted to obstruct justice by facilitating a witness's plan to refuse to comply with a subpoena;

- attempted to obstruct justice by encouraging a witness to file an affidavit that the President knew would be false, and then by making use of that false affidavit at his own deposition;

- lied to potential grand jury witnesses, knowing that they would repeat those lies before the grand jury; and

- engaged in a pattern of conduct that was inconsistent with his constitutional duty to faithfully execute the laws.

The evidence shows that these acts, and others, were part of a pattern that began as an effort to prevent the disclosure of information about the President's relationship with a former

White House intern and employee, Monica S. Lewinsky, and continued as an effort to prevent the information from being disclosed in an ongoing criminal investigation.

FACTUAL BACKGROUND

In May 1994, Paula Corbin Jones filed a lawsuit against William Jefferson Clinton in the United States District Court for the Eastern District of Arkansas. Ms. Jones alleged that while he was the Governor of Arkansas, President Clinton sexually harassed her during an incident in a Little Rock hotel room. President Clinton denied the allegations. He also challenged the ability of a private litigant to pursue a lawsuit against a sitting President. In May 1997, the Supreme Court unanimously rejected the President's legal argument. The Court concluded that Ms. Jones, "[l]ike every other citizen who properly invokes [the District Court's] jurisdiction . . . has a right to an orderly disposition of her claims," and that therefore Ms. Jones was entitled to pursue her claims while the President was in office. . . .

One sharply disputed issue in the *Jones* litigation was the extent to which the President would be required to disclose information about sexual relationships he may have had with "other women." . . .

In late 1997, the issue was presented to United States District Judge Susan Webber Wright for resolution. Judge Wright's decision was unambiguous. For purposes of pretrial discovery, President Clinton was required to provide certain information about his alleged relationships with other women. . . .

In mid-December 1997, the President answered one of the written discovery questions posed by Ms. Jones on this issue. When asked to identify all women who were state or federal employees and with whom he had had "sexual relations" since

1986, the President answered under oath: "None." For purposes of this interrogatory, the term "sexual relations" was not defined.

On January 17, 1998, President Clinton was questioned under oath about his relationships with other women in the workplace, this time at a deposition. Judge Wright presided over the deposition. The President was asked numerous questions about his relationship with Monica Lewinsky, by then a 24-year-old former White House intern, White House employee, and Pentagon employee. Under oath and in the presence of Judge Wright, the President denied that he had engaged in a "sexual affair," a "sexual relationship," or "sexual relations" with Ms. Lewinsky. The President also stated that he had no specific memory of having been alone with Ms. Lewinsky, that he remembered few details of any gifts they might have exchanged, and indicated that no one except his attorneys had kept him informed of Ms. Lewinsky's status as a potential witness in the *Jones* case.

THE INVESTIGATION

On January 12, 1998, this Office received information that Monica Lewinsky was attempting to influence the testimony of one of the witnesses in the *Jones* litigation, and that Ms. Lewinsky herself was prepared to provide false information under oath in that lawsuit. The OIC was also informed that Ms. Lewinsky had spoken to the President and the President's close friend Vernon Jordan about being subpoenaed to testify in the *Jones* suit, and that Vernon Jordan and others were helping her find a job. . . .

After gathering preliminary evidence to test the information's reliability, the OIC presented the evidence to Attorney General Janet Reno. Based on her review of the information, the Attorney General determined that a further investigation by the Independent Counsel was required.

. . . On April 1, 1998, Judge Wright granted President Clinton's motion for summary judgment, concluding that even if the facts alleged by Paula Jones were true, her claims failed as a matter of law. Ms. Jones has filed an appeal, and as of the date of this Referral, the matter remains under consideration by the United States Court of Appeals for the Eighth Circuit.

After the dismissal of Ms. Jones's lawsuit, the criminal investigation continued. It was (and is) the view of this Office that any attempt to obstruct the proper functioning of the judicial system, regardless of the perceived merits of the underlying case, is a serious matter that warrants further inquiry. After careful consideration of all the evidence, the OIC has concluded that the evidence of wrongdoing is substantial and credible, and that the wrongdoing is of sufficient gravity that it warrants referral to Congress.

THE SIGNIFICANCE OF THE EVIDENCE OF WRONGDOING

It is not the role of this Office to determine whether the President's actions warrant impeachment by the House and removal by the Senate; those judgments are, of course, constitutionally entrusted to the legislative branch. This Office is authorized, rather, to conduct criminal investigations and to seek criminal prosecutions for matters within its jurisdiction. In carrying out its investigation, however, this Office also has a statutory duty to disclose to Congress information that "may constitute grounds for an impeachment," a task that inevitably requires judgment about the seriousness of the acts revealed by the evidence.

From the beginning, this phase of the OIC's investigation

has been criticized as an improper inquiry into the President's personal behavior; indeed, the President himself suggested that specific inquiries into his conduct were part of an effort to "criminalize my private life." The regrettable fact that the investigation has often required witnesses to discuss sensitive personal matters has fueled this perception.

All Americans, including the President, are entitled to enjoy a private family life, free from public or governmental scrutiny. But the privacy concerns raised in this case are subject to limits, three of which we briefly set forth here.

First. The first limit was imposed when the President was sued in federal court for alleged sexual harassment. The evidence in such litigation is often personal. . . . Nevertheless, Congress and the Supreme Court have concluded that embarrassment-related concerns must give way to the greater interest in allowing aggrieved parties to pursue their claims. . . .

Second. The second limit was imposed when Judge Wright required disclosure of the precise information that is in part the subject of this Referral. A federal judge specifically ordered the President, on more than one occasion, to provide the requested information about relationships with other women, including Monica Lewinsky. . . . Perjury and attempts to obstruct the gathering of evidence can never be an acceptable response to a court order, regardless of the eventual course or outcome of the litigation.

The Supreme Court has spoken forcefully about perjury and other forms of obstruction of justice:

> In this constitutional process of securing a witness' testimony, perjury simply has no place whatever. Perjured testimony is an obvious and flagrant affront to the basic concepts of judicial proceedings. Effective restraints against this type of egregious offense are therefore imperative.

Third. The third limit is unique to the President. "The Presidency is more than an executive responsibility. It is the inspiring symbol of all that is highest in American purpose and ideals." When he took the Oath of Office in 1993 and again in 1997, President Clinton swore that he would "faithfully execute the Office of President." As the head of the Executive Branch, the President has the constitutional duty to "take Care that the Laws be faithfully executed." The President gave his testimony in the *Jones* case under oath and in the presence of a federal judge, a member of a co-equal branch of government; he then testified before a federal grand jury, a body of citizens who had themselves taken an oath to seek the truth. In view of the enormous trust and responsibility attendant to his high Office, the President has a manifest duty to ensure that his conduct at all times complies with the law of the land.

In sum, perjury and acts that obstruct justice by any citizen—whether in a criminal case, a grand jury investigation, a congressional hearing, a civil trial, or civil discovery—are profoundly serious matters. When such acts are committed by the President of the United States, we believe those acts "may constitute grounds for an impeachment."

THE SCOPE OF THE REFERRAL

. . . From the outset, it was our strong desire to complete all phases of the investigation before deciding whether to submit to Congress information—if any—that may constitute grounds for an impeachment. But events and the statutory command of Section 595(c) have dictated otherwise. As the investigation into the President's actions with respect to Ms. Lewinsky and the *Jones* litigation progressed, it became apparent that there was a significant body of substantial and credible information that met the Section 595(c) threshold. . . .

THE CONTENTS OF THE REFERRAL

The Referral consists of several parts. Part One is a Narrative. It begins with an overview of the information relevant to this investigation, then sets forth that information in chronological sequence. A large part of the Narrative is devoted to a description of the President's relationship with Monica Lewinsky. The nature of the relationship was the subject of many of the President's false statements, and his desire to keep the relationship secret provides a motive for many of his actions that apparently were designed to obstruct justice.

The Narrative is lengthy and detailed. It is the view of this Office that the details are crucial to an informed evaluation of the testimony, the credibility of witnesses, and the reliability of other evidence. Many of the details reveal highly personal information; many are sexually explicit. This is unfortunate, but it is essential. The President's defense to many of the allegations is based on a close parsing of the definitions that were used to describe his conduct. . . .

Part Two of the Referral is entitled "Information that May Constitute Grounds for An Impeachment." This "Grounds" portion of the Referral summarizes the specific evidence that the President lied under oath and attempted to obstruct justice. . . .

Articles of Impeachment Against William Jefferson Clinton, Passed by the House of Representatives Committee on the Judiciary (December 16, 1998)

Based on the information presented in the Starr Report and its own fact-finding, the House Judiciary Committee approved four articles of impeachment against President Clinton. Clinton's defenders maintained that he committed no underlying crime, making whatever misconduct he engaged in not serious enough for impeachment. His opponents argued that Clinton's actions constituted an abuse of power that undermined his oath of office. Ultimately, in the full vote of the House, only the first and third articles passed, accusing Clinton of perjury and obstruction of justice. Under these mostly party-line votes, Clinton became just the second president in American history to be impeached.

RESOLUTION

Impeaching William Jefferson Clinton, President of the United States, for high crimes and misdemeanors.

ARTICLE I (*PASSED BY FULL HOUSE OF REPRESENTATIVES)

William Jefferson Clinton, in violation of his constitutional oath faithfully to execute the office of President of the United States . . . has willfully corrupted and manipulated the judicial process of the United States for his personal gain and exoneration, impeding the administration of justice, in that:

On August 17, 1998, William Jefferson Clinton swore to tell the truth, the whole truth, and nothing but the truth before a Federal grand jury of the United States. Contrary to that oath, William Jefferson Clinton willfully provided perjurious, false and misleading testimony to the grand jury concerning one or more of the following: (1) the nature and details of his relationship with a subordinate Government employee; (2) prior perjurious, false and misleading testimony he gave in a Federal civil rights action brought against him; (3) prior false and misleading statements he allowed his attorney to make to a Federal judge in that civil rights action; and (4) his corrupt efforts to influence the testimony of witnesses and to impede the discovery of evidence in that civil rights action. . . .

ARTICLE II

William Jefferson Clinton . . . has willfully corrupted and manipulated the judicial process of the United States for his personal gain and exoneration, impeding the administration of justice, in that:

(1) William Jefferson Clinton, in sworn answers to written questions asked as part of a Federal civil rights action

brought against him, willfully provided perjurious, false and misleading testimony in response to questions deemed relevant by a Federal judge concerning conduct and proposed conduct with subordinate employees.

(2) William Jefferson Clinton . . . willfully provided perjurious, false and misleading testimony in response to questions deemed relevant by a Federal judge concerning the nature and details of his relationship with a subordinate Government employee, his knowledge of that employee's involvement and participation in the civil rights action brought against him, and his corrupt efforts to influence the testimony of that employee. . . .

ARTICLE III (*PASSED BY FULL HOUSE OF REPRESENTATIVES)

William Jefferson Clinton . . . has prevented, obstructed, and impeded the administration of justice, and has to that end engaged personally, and through his subordinates and agents, in a course of conduct or scheme designed to delay, impede, cover up, and conceal the existence of evidence and testimony related to a Federal civil rights action brought against him in a duly instituted judicial proceeding.

The means used to implement this course of conduct or scheme included one or more of the following acts:

(1) William Jefferson Clinton corruptly encouraged a witness in a Federal civil rights action brought against him to execute a sworn affidavit in that proceeding that he knew to be perjurious, false and misleading.

(2) William Jefferson Clinton corruptly encouraged a witness in a Federal civil rights action brought against him to give perjurious, false and misleading testimony . . .

(3) William Jefferson Clinton corruptly engaged in, encouraged, or supported a scheme to conceal evidence that had been subpoenaed in a Federal civil rights action brought against him.

(4) William Jefferson Clinton intensified and succeeded in an effort to secure job assistance to a witness in a Federal civil rights action brought against him in order to corruptly prevent the truthful testimony of that witness . . .

(5) William Jefferson Clinton corruptly allowed his attorney to make false and misleading statements to a Federal judge characterizing an affidavit, in order to prevent questioning deemed relevant by the judge. . . .

(6) William Jefferson Clinton related a false and misleading account of events relevant to a Federal civil rights action brought against him to a potential witness in that proceeding, in order to corruptly influence the testimony of that witness.

(7) William Jefferson Clinton made false and misleading statements to potential witnesses in a Federal grand jury proceeding in order to corruptly influence the testimony of those witnesses. . . .

ARTICLE IV

William Jefferson Clinton . . . has contravened the authority of the legislative branch and the truth seeking purpose of a coordinate investigative proceeding, in that, as President, William Jefferson Clinton refused and failed to respond to certain written requests for admission and willfully made perjurious, false and misleading sworn statements in response to certain written requests for admission propounded to him as part of the impeachment inquiry. . . . William Jefferson Clinton, in refusing and failing to respond and in making perjurious, false and misleading statements, assumed to himself functions and judgments necessary to the exercise of the sole power of impeachment vested by the Constitution in the House of Representatives and exhibited contempt for the inquiry. . . .

"Post-Impeachment Speech,"
by Bill Clinton
(December 20, 1998)

In this speech, delivered soon after the House voted to proceed with impeachment, President Clinton calls the impeachment a partisan affair that is destructive to American governance. He accepts responsibility for his wrongdoing, but like his congressional defenders, argues that his transgressions do not warrant the grave punishment of impeachment and removal. Clinton tries to bring the country's focus back to his policies and to end the rancor around his presidency. Still, for the following months, the Senate impeachment trial would consume his presidency.

Let me begin by expressing my profound and heartfelt thanks to Congressman Gephardt and the leadership and all the members of the Democratic caucus for what they did today.

I thank the few brave Republicans who withstood enormous pressures to stand with them for the plain meaning of the Constitution and for the proposition that we need to pull together, to move beyond partisanship, to get on with the business of our country.

I thank the millions upon millions of American citizens who

have expressed their support and their friendship to Hillary, to me, to our family, and to our administration during these last several weeks. . . .

The question is, what are we going to do now? I have accepted responsibility for what I did wrong in my personal life, and I have invited members of Congress to work with us to find a reasonable bipartisan and proportionate response.

That approach was rejected today by Republicans in the House, but I hope it will be embraced by the Senate. I hope there will be a constitutional and fair means of resolving this matter in a prompt manner.

Meanwhile, I will continue to do the work of the American people. . . . We have a lot to do before we enter the 21st century.

And we still have to keep working to build that elusive one America I have talked so much about.

For six years now, I have done everything I could to bring our country together across the lines that divide us, including bringing Washington together across party lines. Out in the country, people are pulling together. But just as America is coming together, it must look—from the country's point of view—like Washington is coming apart. . . .

We must stop the politics of personal destruction.

We must get rid of the poisonous venom of excessive partisanship, obsessive animosity and uncontrolled anger.

That is not what America deserves. That is not what America is about. . . . We are a good and decent country but we have significant challenges we have to face.

In order to do it right, we have to have some atmosphere of decency and civility, some presumption of good faith. . . .

We need a constructive debate that has all the different voices in this country heard in the halls of Congress.

I want the American people to know today that I am still committed to working with people of good faith and good will of both parties to do what's best for our country, to bring our nation together, to lift our people up, to move us all forward together.

It's what I've tried to do for six years. It's what I intend to do for two more until the last hour of the last day of my term.

So with profound gratitude for the defense of the Constitution and the best in America that was raised today by the members here and those who joined them, I ask the American people to move with me—to go on from here to rise above the rancor, to overcome the pain and division, to be a repairer of the breach—all of us—to make this country as one America what it can and must be for our children in the new century about to dawn. Thank you very much.

"Speech on Censure Resolution," by Dianne Feinstein (February 12, 1999)

Bill Clinton's Senate trial was less dramatic than Andrew Johnson's. Though the debate was filled with partisan vitriol and serious accusations, the conviction vote was never close to passing. Forty-five Republicans voted for the perjury charge and fifty-five Republicans voted for the obstruction of justice charge. No Democrats joined them for either vote, however, meaning the Senate fell far short of the sixty-seven votes needed for removal. Still, some senators sought a different approach, one that acknowledged Clinton's wrongdoing without saying it warranted impeachment: congressional censure. Dianne Feinstein, a member of Clinton's own party, led the Senate push to censure Clinton for conduct that she believed was beneath the presidency. Her effort failed, however, with not enough Democrats willing to so harshly criticize their own president. To date, Andrew Jackson is the only president ever to have been censured—and even that censure was expunged three years after it was approved. In this speech, she addresses the presiding officer of the Senate, referred to as "Mr. President."

Mr. President, I just want to point out to everyone who is interested that a censure resolution has been entered at the desk. It has 38 cosponsors.

Mr. President, during these trying days, the question has been asked of many of us: "What will we tell our children about this sordid period in our Nation's history?"

Mr. President, Members of the Senate, I had hoped to be able to tell my granddaughter and, indeed, the rest of our Nation, that the United States Senate had come together in bipartisan fellowship to approve a censure resolution that would deliver a clear message that the behavior of President William Jefferson Clinton has been inappropriate, intolerable and unacceptable.

Unfortunately, some in this body have forestalled our ability to bring such a resolution to the floor of the Senate for a vote. This I regret deeply.

There are moments in history when we are able to rise up against the forces driving us apart and come together with a united purpose. I believe that the censure resolution provided us with just such an opportunity.

While not a cure-all, the resolution is a way to share with our children and the rest of our nation our findings, our sentiments, our belief that the actions of the President are a violation of the trust of the American people and have brought shame and dishonor upon the presidency and the man. . . .

Over the past few weeks, I have worked very closely with a large number of Senators to develop a bipartisan resolution, largely because I felt it so important that anyone who looks at this shabby episode of American history understands that while one may not vote to convict and remove a President, one can have profound dismay and concern about the misconduct that was inherent in the articles of impeachment.

. . . Earlier today, I voted against conviction and removal of the President on both articles of impeachment. I did not believe the House managers established beyond a reasonable doubt that this President is guilty of perjury and obstruction of justice.

Although I deplore the circumstances that have brought us to this point, I do not believe they present a clear and present danger to the functioning of our government, and therefore this President, who has been a good President for the people of the United States, should not be convicted and removed from office.

However, I feel very strongly and sincerely that the acquittal of the President on the articles of impeachment should not be the Senate's last word on the President's conduct, and that without further action such as a resolution of censure, the wrong message about the President's actions and the Senate's views thereon will be sent to the country. . . .

INTENT BEHIND THE
CENSURE RESOLUTION

I want to clear up once and for all the intent behind our censure resolution.

The resolution does not express legal conclusions in the court of impeachment. Rather, it is a legislative measure, expressing our conclusions regarding the President's conduct.

The legal conclusions to be made in this case, if any, will be left to a court of law. Our intent is not to bind or influence the court one way or another, for good or ill, in making any determinations which it may about the President's conduct.

Instead, our purpose is to speak to the moral ramifications of the President's conduct, and to the message that those actions send to the people of our nation, especially its youth.

While the President's actions do not constitute a fundamental threat to the nation, neither were they at all acceptable.

The President's conduct was both willful and wrong, clearly by any standard, his behavior is indefensible.

These actions demeaned the Office of the President, violated the trust of the American people, and brought shame and dishonor upon President Clinton. . . .

. . . I am very pleased that we have been joined by a very significant number of co-sponsors from both sides of the aisle. These co-sponsors run the ideological gamut from liberal to moderate to conservative. The breadth of these co-sponsors, I believe, represents the widespread consensus that the President's actions merit serious condemnation. . . .

HISTORICAL PRECEDENTS FOR CENSURE

Censure is an extraordinary measure that Congress has used sparingly over the past 200 hundred years.

Censure is rare because it is such a powerful expression of Congressional criticism. In a censure resolution, a House of Congress publicly states its collective view that an individual has acted beyond the bounds of acceptable professional conduct. A censure records for history the major misdoings of public men and women.

Over the past 200 years, the House and Senate have initiated censure proceedings against Executive Branch officials on at least 13 different occasions.

Three times a House of Congress has adopted measures that could be described as a censure of a President. In 1834, the Senate censured President Andrew Jackson. Twice the House has adopted statements criticizing Presidents—in the cases of John Tyler and James Buchanan.

Censuring President Clinton would be consistent with historical use of this rare, but powerful, Congressional power. . . .

BIPARTISAN CENSURE
PROMOTES HEALING

In this bipartisan censure, we provided the Senate with a real opportunity to achieve a strong, unifying, bipartisan conclusion to this whole tawdry, exhausting and divisive controversy. . . .

The Senate started its proceedings on a high note, when we came together to agree unanimously, across party lines, upon procedures for the trial. Passing our censure resolution by a strong, bipartisan vote would represent an appropriate "bookend" to this bipartisan beginning, and would stand this Senate well in the annals of history.

Moreover, it would put the proper historical perspective upon the Senate's actions and determinations, which should not be read as a vindication of the President.

I believe that passing this censure on a bipartisan basis would bring a real closure to the process, and would help to heal the divisions between the parties which were created during these proceedings, so that we can move on to work together to address the real problems confronting the American people, like saving social security, improving education, and continuing the fight to reduce crime. . . .

RESOLUTION OF CENSURE

Whereas William Jefferson Clinton, President of the United States, engaged in an inappropriate relationship with a subordinate employee in the White House, which was shameful, reckless and indefensible;

Whereas William Jefferson Clinton, President of the United States, deliberately misled and deceived the American people, and people in all branches of the United States government;

Whereas William Jefferson Clinton, President of the United States, gave false or misleading testimony and his actions have had the effect of impeding discovery of evidence in judicial proceedings;

Whereas William Jefferson Clinton's conduct in this matter is unacceptable for a President of the United States, does demean the Office of the President as well as the President himself, and creates disrespect for the laws of the land;

Whereas President Clinton fully deserves censure for engaging in such behavior;

Whereas future generations of Americans must know that such behavior is not only unacceptable but also bears grave consequences, including loss of integrity, trust and respect;

Whereas William Jefferson Clinton remains subject to criminal actions in a court of law like any other citizen;

Whereas William Jefferson Clinton's conduct in this matter has brought shame and dishonor to himself and to the Office of the President; and

Whereas William Jefferson Clinton through his conduct in this matter has violated the trust of the American people:

Now therefore, be it *Resolved*, That the United States Senate does hereby censure William Jefferson Clinton, President of the United States, and does condemn his wrongful conduct in the strongest terms; and now be it

Further resolved, That the United States Senate recognizes the historic gravity of this bipartisan resolution, and trusts and urges that future congresses will recognize the importance of allowing this bipartisan statement of censure and condemnation to remain intact for all time; and be it

Further resolved, That the Senate now move on to other matters of significance to our people, to reconcile differences between and within the branches of government, and to work together—across party lines—for the benefit of the American people.

"A Sitting President's Amenability to Indictment and Criminal Prosecution," by the Office of Legal Counsel (October 16, 2000)

Bill Clinton was not happy about how intrusive independent counsel Ken Starr's investigation had been into his presidency. When the law authorizing independent counsels came up for renewal in 1999, Clinton did not push for its renewal, and the law expired. Yet he had also been scarred by the seemingly endless lawsuits he faced. Under the 1973 Nixon OLC memo, a sitting president could not be criminally indicted. That did not stop the Supreme Court from ruling in Clinton v. Jones *in 1997 that a sitting president can face civil litigation, even for actions taken before becoming president. In 2000, the Clinton administration asked its OLC to review the Nixon memo. In its memo, Clinton's OLC agrees with the prior memo's conclusions, determining that a president cannot be criminally indicted while in office—a decision that remains Justice Department policy today.*

MEMORANDUM OPINION FOR
THE ATTORNEY GENERAL

In 1973, the Department concluded that the indictment or criminal prosecution of a sitting President would impermissibly undermine the capacity of the executive branch to perform its constitutionally assigned functions. . . . We believe that the conclusion reached by the Department in 1973 still represents the best interpretation of the Constitution.

The Department's consideration of this issue in 1973 arose in two distinct legal contexts. First, the Office of Legal Counsel . . . prepared a comprehensive memorandum in the fall of 1973 that analyzed whether all federal civil officers are immune from indictment or criminal prosecution while in office, and, if not, whether the President and Vice President in particular are immune from indictment or criminal prosecution while in office. . . . The OLC memorandum concluded that all federal civil officers except the President are subject to indictment and criminal prosecution while still in office; the President is uniquely immune from such process.

In this memorandum, we conclude that the determinations made by the Department in 1973, both in the OLC memorandum and in the Solicitor General's brief, remain sound and that subsequent developments in the law validate both the analytical framework applied and the conclusions reached at that time. In Part I, we describe in some detail the Department's 1973 analysis and conclusions. In Part II, we examine more recent Supreme Court case law and conclude that it comports with the Department's 1973 conclusions . . .